Praise for
Reconciliation in Afghanistan

"Michael Semple's Reconciliation in Afghanistan *is based on a vast knowledge of the country and many discussions with the members of the Taliban. It is the best blueprint available about how to accomplish the complex and very necessary task of bringing 'reconcilable' Taliban into ordinary Afghan politics, arguing that it is far from impossible, but appropriately underlining the many obstacles that will be encountered on the way to this goal. Semple's study is deeply researched and well calibrated in its analyses and judgments."*

—Peter Bergen, author of *Holy War, Inc.* and *The Osama bin Laden I Know*

"Both President Obama and President Karzai have embraced reconciliation with insurgents ready to enter the Afghan political process as an important element in their strategy to stabilize that country. Michael Semple offers a lucid, supremely well-informed, and compelling exposition of peacemaking in Afghanistan. He reveals the many attempts to date at co-opting and accommodating elements of the Taliban opposition. He explains why these efforts have generally had little impact to date, sets out what can reasonably be expected from such a process, and recommends a well-considered way forward."

—Ambassador James Dobbins, America's first post-9/11 special envoy for Afghanistan and author of *After the Taliban: Nation Building in Afghanistan*

"This study presents an excellent illustration of the diversity of the groups and networks that are grouped under the term Taliban by the media and inexperienced analysts. Reconciliation in Afghanistan *is well conceived and well written. It effectively suggests series of steps Afghans, the United States, and the international community might take as they all seek to turn a new page in the efforts to address the security and stability issues that continue to plague Afghanistan and the region."*

—Thomas E. Gouttierre, Center for Afghanistan Studies, University of Nebraska at Omaha

"As the Obama administration develops and implements its revised strategy on Afghanistan and Pakistan, a principal topic of debate is "reconciliation"—how to deal politically with Taliban and other insurgents who are not pursuing al-Qaeda's global objectives in search of a political solution. Michael Semple brings to bear a wealth of practical experience on the ground in Pakistan and Afghanistan. He has spoken in-depth with more insurgent commanders than virtually any international official, and his long service in the region has equipped him with the knowledge, language skills, and personal networks to analyze such contacts in depth. The result is the most detailed and knowledgeable road map to date for how to pursue dialogue and negotiation with Taliban and other Islamist guerrillas in the area that are today sheltering the leadership of al-Qaeda."

—Barnett R. Rubin, Center on International Cooperation, New York University

"This invaluable book offers a perspective on reconciliation that is available nowhere else in the literature on the subject. The author's comprehensive, balanced, and objective review of reconciliation initiatives and their effectiveness indicate a familiarity with his subject that is unmatched. Semple goes well beyond merely examining approaches to reconciliation in providing the context necessary to understand why various strategies may have greater or lesser success."

—Marvin Weinbaum, Middle East Institute

Reconciliation in Afghanistan

Reconciliation in Afghanistan

Michael Semple

UNITED STATES INSTITUTE OF PEACE PRESS
Washington, DC

UNITED STATES INSTITUTE OF PEACE
1200 17th Street NW, Suite 200
Washington, DC 20036-3011
www.usip.org

Library of Congress Cataloging-in-Publication Data

Semple, Michael.
  Reconciliation in Afghanistan / Michael Semple.
     p. cm.
  ISBN 978-1-60127-042-9 (pbk)
  1. Reconciliation—Political aspects—Afghanistan. 2. Conflict management—Afghanistan. 3. Peace-building—Afghanistan.
  4. Afghanistan—Politics and government—2001. I. Title.
  DS371.4.S36 2009
  958.104'7—dc22
                              2009015351

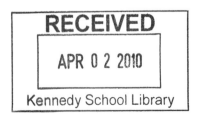

Contents

Abbreviations

ANA	Afghan National Army
ANAP	Afghan National Auxiliary Police
ANSF	Afghan National Security Forces
FATA	Federally Administered Tribal Areas
ICRC	International Committee of the Red Cross
IED	Improvised Explosive Device
ISAF	International Security Assistance Force
JUI	Jamiat Ulema Islami (Pakistan's Assembly of Islamic Clergy)
NDS	National Directorate of Security (Afghan Intelligence Service I formerly referred to as Khad)
NSC	National Security Council
NWFP	North-West Frontier Province
PAG	Policy Action Group
PDPA	People's Democratic Party of Afghanistan
PRT	Provincial Reconstruction Team
PTS	Proceayee Tahqeem Solha (Strengthening Peace Program)
UNAMA	United Nations Assistance Mission in Afghanistan

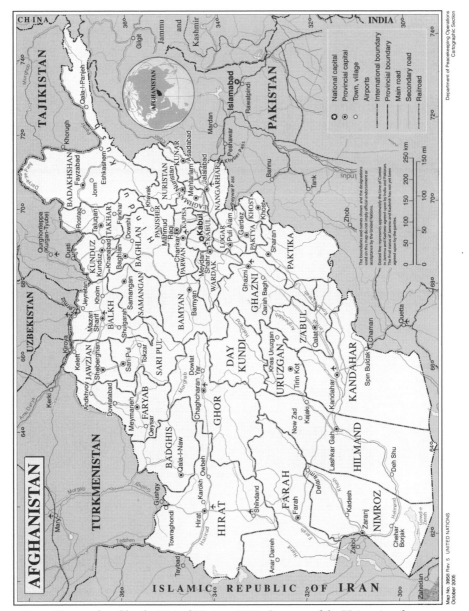

Source: Map produced by the United Nations, 2005. Courtesy of the University of
Texas Libraries, University of Texas at Austin.

Introduction

The current Afghan political system was established through the Bonn Accords in 2001. At the time of the framing of the accords, it was widely hoped that the rapid collapse of the Taliban regime and the installation of a broad-based, internationally backed administration would bring an end to large-scale conflict in Afghanistan. The accords made reference to the idea of reconciliation,[1] and the political road map outlined in them included measures with significant potential to further a process of reconciliation. The accords' first substantive paragraph reaffirms participants' determination to "end the tragic conflict in Afghanistan and promote *national reconciliation*, lasting peace, stability and respect for human rights in the country."[2] Indeed, the informal script, articulated both by Afghan leaders associated with the post-2001 dispensation and by international supporters, was that the Bonn process represented a transition from a twenty-three-year conflict (1978–2001) to a new era of peace in which the accords' implementation would launch a process of social, economic, and institutional renewal in a post-conflict environment. In short, reconciliation pursued within Afghanistan's post-conflict context was meant to create the foundations on which a lasting peace would rest.

In this sense, reconciliation was expected to help secure a tentative, preexisting peace. The Interim and Transitional Authorities represented a common space, accessible to all Afghans, within which they could effect their reconciliation. This peace and reconciliation script was attractive, offering a source of both domestic and international legitimacy to the process. The administration could present itself to Afghans as a government of national unity whose role was to deliver the peace that had proved elusive since the failed transition from Communist rule in 1992. Similarly, international partners could present themselves as

---

1. This paper uses the term reconciliation to mean nonviolent, political engagement with or between conflicting parties with the intent of rendering possible and then establishing a peaceful relationship between them.

2. United Nations, "Agreement on Provisional Arrangements in Afghanistan Pending the Re-establishment of Permanent Government Institutions," December 2001, http://www.un.org/News/dh/latest/afghan/afghan-agree.htm (accessed March 21, 2009); italics added.

1

peacebuilders through the UN-sanctioned stabilization of post-conflict Afghanistan. This idea of pursuing reconciliation only after fighting has stopped—that is, to consolidate peace and prevent future conflict—has plenty of international parallels. Examples of such post-conflict reconciliation processes include those witnessed in Cambodia, Northern Ireland, Rwanda, South Africa, and even the countries affected by the Second World War. In these cases, reconciliation meant altering the relations between the parties to the conflict and other citizens to provide a basis for coexistence.[3]

The Bonn Accords anticipated an "interim" and "transitional" period until the full establishment of representative Afghan political institutions. With the convening of Parliament after the 2005 elections, therefore, the transitional period—and with it the Bonn process—came to an end. But in today's post-Bonn period, Afghanistan faces a new round of conflict associated with the insurgency that arose in 2003 and escalated most sharply after 2005. Although a revived interest in reconciliation has accompanied this resurgence of conflict, the current situation warrants rethinking the very idea of reconciliation in Afghanistan and how it might be operational there. Unlike during the Bonn process, the concept of reconciliation is presently being invoked in the context of a search for peaceful, political approaches that will stabilize a deteriorating situation—that is, win the war.

This new expectation of reconciliation amid active conflict implies both stopping the fighting and creating permanent peaceful relationships, reversing the trend toward adversarial ones. But the conflict itself has altered relations among the actors. The Afghan government, which could originally style itself as an inclusive, accessible national authority, is now clearly a party to the conflict. And the insurgents "targeted" for reconciliation insist that their main fight is not with other Afghans but with the government's international backers who had hoped their role would be that of supporting the government in pursuing reconciliation. Because the situation on the ground has changed and a full-scale insur-

---

3. "Reconciliation . . . not only tries to find solutions to the issues underlying the conflict but also works to alter the adversaries' relationships from that of resentment and hostility to friendship and harmony." Hizkias Assefa, "The Meaning of Reconciliation," in *People Building Peace: 35 Inspiring Stories from Around the World*, ed. Paul van Tongeren et al. (Utrecht: European Platform for Conflict Prevention and Transformation, 1999).

gency is now underway, the roles of key actors pursuing reconciliation and the content of programs to give practical shape to reconciliation must be revised.

This monograph investigates the historical and political context to the contemporary debate on reconciliation in Afghanistan. It outlines approaches to reconciliation adopted in phases of the conflict prior to 2001, considers the extent to which the architecture of the Bonn process provided a basis for reconciliation, and describes the failure of efforts to establish a lasting peace after 2001 and the development of the insurgency. It also offers empirical evidence on the limited extent to which figures from the Taliban regime were reconciled during the Bonn process, provides a political analysis of the Taliban movement, and identifies aspects of the post-2001 strategy pursued by the Afghan government and international community that contributed to the development of the insurgency. It then reviews the range of initiatives that have been pursued since 2001 to promote the reconciliation of those who are in armed opposition to the Afghan government and its international allies, suggests lessons learned from these initiatives that should be applied in any realistic reconciliation strategy for Afghanistan, and examines the support that the international community has given to various reconciliation processes in the country. It concludes by summarizing key findings and offers realistic recommendations to both the Afghan government and the international community in their pursuit of achieving reconciliation in Afghanistan.

The monograph's recommendations for building a realistic reconciliation strategy are based on its finding that the current insurgency is not monolithic but rather a loose association of different commander networks that have some overlapping interests but that also have varying degrees of adherence to the leadership of the Taliban movement. Although the monograph argues that the prospects of a general political agreement between the Afghan government and the insurgency are poor, it finds that there is potential for the reconciliation of particular commander networks. To date, however, reconciliation efforts by the Afghan government—and international support for such efforts—have been inadequate. If even modest progress is to be made in reconciliation in Afghanistan, the arrangements for integrating reconciled commanders must first be overhauled and complementary efforts that will improve Afghan governance and strengthen security structures must first be made.

Origins of the Study

Over a three-year period between 2004 and 2007, the author conducted face-to-face meetings with some two hundred Afghans who were involved directly or indirectly in the country's insurgency.[4] The men who came to these meetings ranged from senior figures in the Taliban leadership to the lowest level of active insurgent. Some contacts commanded local fronts with dozens of fighters, and at least one commanded all fighters in a province. Meeting participants also included former ministers, provincial governors, mid-level functionaries from the Taliban regime, veteran mujahideen fighters of doubtful loyalty, and dozens of young men who had been foot soldiers during the Taliban regime but who had found themselves elevated to the status of commander. What all of them clearly had in common was not just a willingness to talk—but a willingness to talk to a Westerner.

This fact in itself was sometimes surprising, as many of the young men were remarkably frank in describing their involvement in armed action against NATO and Afghan government forces. They described being bombed and shot at and losing comrades and stepping into the shoes of slain commanders with a disarming matter-of-factness. They also all came across as Afghans with a stake in the affairs of their country. The young men involved in the fighting had an obvious sense of belonging to their network of comrades even if they could not give an altogether plausible account of why the network was active in the insurgency. Despite this, the tales that the fighters told about the events of 2002 and 2003 and how, despite initial hopes that they could live in peace, they were driven to join the incipient insurgency were at the same time plausible and tragicomic. Many of the men expressed their aspirations for the future, and none of them came across as crazy or fanatic.

---

4. Meetings were undertaken in the author's capacity as deputy to the European Union special representative for Afghanistan, under a section of his mandate calling for support to the Afghan government's reconciliation process.

Of course, some interlocutors were what one might call tactical players—that is, they were simply checking out what advantage might be gained by talking to government or Westerners while keeping their real intentions to themselves. But even this kind of tactical play is a well-established part of Afghan social and political behavior, described in every historical account of the country. None of the interlocutors seemed to be a puppet or slave of a foreign power. Some of them did talk openly about patterns of regional interference, principally in their descriptions of assistance that they had received from Pakistani intelligence agents. But even if they acknowledged receiving such assistance, none of the insurgents appeared wedded to an agenda dictated by such sponsors. Although fighters displayed a certain amount of bravado when boasting of their firefights with NATO, they seemed quite happy to accept that the countries in NATO wanted to help Afghans rebuild their country. The common ground that was reached in almost all of the conversations was that there would be no purely military solution to confrontation in Afghanistan and that peace would have to be made.

There are many reasons why conflict persists in Afghanistan. There are also many reasons why insurgents who have taken the initial step of accepting an invitation to a discreet meeting with a political officer have not gone on to reconcile. But the lack of sustained commitment to reconciliation on the part of the Afghan government and its Western backers is a major reason why opportunities for reconciliation have been wasted. The reality discovered by the author—and the two hundred Afghans who took the initiative to talk peace—was that government structures, the Western military and political presence, and the United Nations were all singularly ill-equipped and often disinclined to take the needed steps to enable these Afghans to reconcile and reintegrate peacefully back into society. The collective failure of those engaged in the political process in Afghanistan since 2001 to develop credible alternatives for these men and those like them has led to profound consequences: a disastrous escalation of the conflict, increased questioning of the basis of international engagement in Afghanistan, and a loss of hope that the fall of the Taliban regime might mark the return of peace to Afghanistan.

Rethinking Reconciliation for Afghanistan

The definitions of reconciliation that have been applied to globally prominent post-conflict reconciliation processes may also be relevant to Afghanistan's in-conflict reconciliation efforts. Peter Brecke and William Long define reconciliation as "returning to peace, harmony, or amicable relations after a conflict."[5] In their definition, it becomes operational through a *reconciliation event* in which representatives of the conflicting parties physically come together through public acts and rituals. The Glencree Centre for Reconciliation in Ireland defines reconciliation as a process that embraces four principal "transformations" that move a society from a state of conflict to a state of peace.[6] These transformations include "healing" by those who have suffered from the conflict; "building relationships" among the parties to the conflict; "reconstruction" of physical infrastructure and institutions; and the creation of "interdependence" within the society that has been segmented and compartmentalized by the conflict. In describing reconciliation as conflict prevention through the restoration of relations, Hizkias Assefa envisages the voluntary acknowledgment of responsibility, remorse, and apology; the reduction of enmity; the redress of past grievances; the creation of safeguards against a repetition of violation; and the construction of new positive relations.[7] Reconciliation as a concept that centers on restoring relations has much resonance in Afghanistan.

While peace built on restoring relations is a common thread that runs through Afghan reconciliation experience, it is also important to point out that a wide range of actions in Afghanistan has explicitly been presented as reconciliation efforts or fall within the definition of them. For example, Afghanistan has experience with publicly announced, negotiated deals between warring parties that are comparable to the reconciliation events described in peacebuilding literature. Traditional Afghan reconciliation processes, in which ritual is employed to symbolize the renewal of relationships, are also resonant of the eminently

---

5. Peter Brecke and William Long, "War and Reconciliation" (Working Paper Series #98-1, Georgia Institute of Technology, Advancement of Conflict Resolution Theory and Education, September 1998).

6. Matthew Seebach, *Worlds Apart: Glencree Peace Education Resource Package* (Glencree, Ireland: Glencree Reconciliation Centre, 2004).

7. Assefa, "The Meaning of Reconciliation."

human, restorative element of reconciliation as described in the literature. Even so, secret deals on cooperation brokered by intelligence agencies are arguably just as much a part of Afghan reconciliation experience and arguably more relevant to bringing about reconciliation during an active conflict than processes that have had a higher public profile.

Practitioners of reconciliation who have the goal of ending the war include those who approach the issue from the perspective of "counterinsurgency" rather than from peacebuilding. As an illustration of this contrasting, more blunt approach, all three explicit references to reconciliation in the United States' *Counterinsurgency* manual stress the need to "eliminate," "kill," or "neutralize irreconcilables and extremists."[8] Given the long and rich tradition of duplicity in counterinsurgency and Afghan warfare, there is a significant gray area of actions that a protagonist may present as reconciliation but that are actually tactical moves calculated to gain advantage. In Afghan moral terms, the relevant distinction concerns *ni-at* (intention). Actions based on an intention to deceive are different from those based on a genuine desire to make peace and cannot be a basis for reconciliation, however difficult it may be to establish the intentions of the parties at the outset.

Although this monograph does not address reconciliation processes deliberately directed at subnational conflicts, the informal cadre of traditional Afghan peacemakers who pursue reconciliation in local conflicts offer an important reserve of experience and tools that may at times be applicable to the national-level effort.[9] Indeed, a wide range of approaches has been used in pursuit of reconciliation in Afghanistan. To facilitate a comparative analysis, this monograph focuses on the six key variables that have defined these approaches:

1. *The standing of those being reconciled*—for example, are they significant conflict actors? Is the reconciliation process between the state and nonstate actors, or between nonstate actors?

---

8. U.S. Army, *Counterinsurgency* (Washington, DC: Headquarters of the Army, 2006).

9. For a recent overview of reconciliation and peacemaking in subnational conflicts, see Matt Walden, *Community Peace-building in Afghanistan* (Oxford: OXFAM International, 2008).

2. *The transparency of the process*—for example, is it managed opaquely within the intelligence domain or transparently within the political and diplomatic domain?

3. *The terms of the bargain*—for example, what is the basis and manner on which reconciliation is to be effected?

4. *The inclusiveness of the process*—for example, does the reconciliation embrace individuals and factions, or a broader range of conflict actors?

5. *The instruments of reconciliation*—for example, which tools are used to pursue and encapsulate reconciliation?

6. *The international dimension*—for example, what is the nature of international involvement or support, if any?

In terms of the *standing* of those being reconciled, much of the current focus is on nonstate actors reconciling with the state, while in previous stages of the conflict much of the emphasis was on reconciliation among nonstate actors. In interpreting the standing of Afghan actors involved in a reconciliation process, it is important to remember that the state and nonstate labels are chronically subject to mutation. The successive shifts in alliances and changing military and political fortunes that have characterized the country's power struggles mean that current political actors often define themselves in terms of past standing. As a result, reconciliation between Afghan parties should be seen as reconciliation between contenders in a long-term power struggle, each with a range of sensitivities and expectations that may not be apparent in their current relative positions. In concrete terms, someone today labeled as an insurgent may be a former Afghan prime minister or governor and may think of himself as a peer—or even as an elder—of the government counterparts with whom he is supposed to reconcile. Current reconciliation processes also vary in terms of how close the reconciled parties have been to the conflict. Some initiatives have involved those who were politically linked with the insurgents, while other initiatives have sought to involve those who were more directly involved in the conflict.

The issue of *transparency* is pertinent when contrasting the reconciliation processes that have emerged from the political and diplomatic domain, which generally operate in a transparent manner, and the security domain, which generally operates in an opaque manner. Afghanistan's reconciliation practice includes examples from both domains, with some of them illustrating a disconnect between political, diplomatic, and human rights concerns and security concerns.

Perhaps the one aspect of reconciliation that generates the most current controversy is the *terms of the bargain*, especially in the case of reconciliation between the state and a nonstate actor. Those seeking to sabotage a reconciliation process have targeted it typically on the grounds that the terms of the bargain are unacceptable or illegitimate. Controversy has revolved around the extent to which, to achieve agreement, a state actor in the reconciliation deal compromises on its vital interests. There has been much variation in the terms that have underlined reconciliation arrangements not only in recent Afghan experience but also in recent Pakistani experience, which is often used as a frame of reference for Afghanistan. For example, many observers have criticized the Pakistani government for signing the 2006 Waziristan Accord, which effectively conceded much of North Waziristan Agency to militant control. Likewise, Pakistan's agreements with militants in Swat in 2008 and 2009, which allow a form of sharia-based justice system in the district in exchange for a suspension of military operations there, have been criticized as acts of appeasement. The terms of the bargain—that is, the extent to which the state or dominant actor agrees to compromise on its vital interests—can generally be defined in one of five ways: *subjugation*, *co-option*, *accommodation*, *appeasement*, and *capitulation* (see figure 1).

At one end, *subjugation* is pretty much synonymous with surrender—the defeated fighter submits to the mercy of the state. Under *co-option*, the fighter reconciles without securing any privilege or deal other than being allowed to join the side with which he is reconciling. In short, the fighter accepts the political order status quo in return for liberty or amnesty and does not achieve any negotiated privileges or political change. In *accommodation*, both contending parties shift from their previous positions, with the state actor making negotiated concessions to win the cooperation or end the hostilities of the nonstate actor. Even so, the essence of the political order remains the same; the nonstate actor is accommodated into this order. The greatest controversy has arisen around claimed instances of *appeasement* and even more extreme cases

Figure 1 Terms of the Reconciliation Bargain

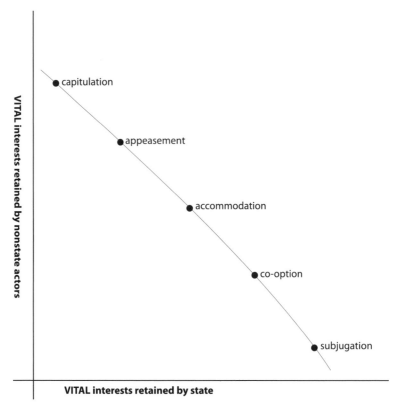

of *capitulation* in which the terms of the bargain favor the nonstate actor. In cases of *appeasement*, the state actor makes major concessions on its vital interests, rolling back on principles that it has hitherto maintained as important, and in return gains only partial concessions from the non-state actor, neither winning a full end to violence nor a guarantee that this will be a final deal. The implication of *appeasement* has always been that its beneficiary will be back for more, leading to eventual *capitulation*, when all vital state interests are compromised.

In terms of *inclusiveness*, recent experience ranges from reconciliation processes that have been designed for a single individual to processes that involve negotiation and reconciliation with a particular warring faction. Others have been more general in scope, offering reconciliation to whole categories of conflict actors. Each process has been based on applying a particular set of tools to transform the relations between the parties effecting reconciliation. The types of nonviolent action used—or *instruments of reconciliation*—have ranged from confidential contacts and negotiations and secret protocols to open political agreements and confidence-building measures and amnesties.

Finally, in terms of the *international dimension*, which concerns the ways in which international actors support or engage with reconciliation initiatives, there was almost a generation's worth of United Nations attempts at achieving reconciliation between the various Afghan parties, beginning with the start of the Soviet intervention and ending with the installation of the Karzai administration. Under the Bonn process, the general mantra of "an Afghan lead" was often applied to reconciliation, leading to the notion that all reconciliation must be Afghan-Afghan, with little more than funding support required from the international community. But the large-scale commitment of international military forces to a counterinsurgency war substantially changes the context of attempts at reconciliation. The United Nations and Western powers no longer have the same nonbelligerent or neutral status that they might have been able to claim in previous phases of the conflict. In short, they are now parties to the conflict.

Given that the focus of this monograph is on reconciliation processes that address the national-level conflict, the obvious question is whether any of the possible reconciliation approaches offer the prospect of achieving a comprehensive settlement and a discrete end to the conflict. Although the political contacts hosted by the government of Saudi Arabia beginning in September 2008 were launched with this very aim, a range of factors indicates that there is little medium-term prospect of any "big bang" reconciliation approach achieving a comprehensive settlement in Afghanistan. Indeed, a general lack of substantive progress should not be surprising given that key actors among the insurgent leadership see advantage in continuing the conflict. Among the mid-level leaders especially there are significant actors who stand to benefit more from ongoing hostilities than from any conceivable political agreement. Additionally, there is no single insurgent organization that could negotiate or enforce an agreement on behalf of the whole insurgency. Furthermore, powerful economic incentives drive the insurgency, including insurgent fundraising and revenue collection, the convergence of organized crime and insurgent networks, and the link between the narcotics trade and the insurgency in Taliban-dominated areas.

Even for those insurgent actors who might plausibly be interested in a political settlement, their assessments of their relative strengths in the current situation differ radically from the assessments informing the government position. Thus, even if one were to conceive of some constellation of insurgent leaders trying to negotiate a comprehensive deal, the gulf between what the insurgents' minimum expectations from any arrangement with the government might be and what the government might conceivably be prepared to offer seems unlikely to be bridged in the near future. Only long-term change in these underlying factors could create the conditions in which general reconciliation would become a realistic possibility. As a result, reconciliation initiatives should be modest in scope, engaging some of the conflict actors and contributing to conflict management but not promising an imminent comprehensive peace settlement.

Past Examples of Reconciliation in Afghanistan

In considering reconciliation processes and instruments, parties to the current Afghan conflict are able to draw on a wide range of historical experience, with examples of both successes and failures. The legacy of reconciliation in Afghanistan includes traditions that have both been drawn upon in all eras and pursued as statecraft by previous administrations. Indeed, given the country's long history of internal and external conflict, the pursuit of reconciliation can be said to be integral to Afghan statecraft and local practice of war. The rituals that are acted out and institutions that are invoked during traditional reconciliation are a core part of Afghan cultural heritage.

Instruments of reconciliation are an especially integral part of the Pashtoon cultural code, known as Pakthunwali. For example, the concept of truce is covered by the custom of *tiga*, or placing the stone.[1] (The Farsi equivalent of this Pashto concept is *sang mandan*.) Per custom, two opposing parties engaged in conflict usually consent to "place the stone" upon the intervention of an elder or respected traditional peacemaker. In so doing, the belligerents are obliged to pause their current fighting and to desist from revenge taking for losses that they have incurred, providing an opportunity for the mediator (which may be a *jirga*, or authorized delegation or forum) to seek a permanent settlement to the conflict. The president explicitly invoked the concept of *tiga* after heavy clashes in Gardez in 2002 between supporters of newly appointed governor Padshah Khan Zadran and a local party opposing his installation, led by Saifullah Ahmadzai.

Another set of traditions relates to the process of belligerents establishing loyalty to a newly dominant power. Such reconciliation instruments may be invoked in case of capitulation, when combatants of a defeated power demonstrate that they have withdrawn from hostilities and adjusted to the new reality. Cases of capitulation have been

---

1. Syed Fida Yunas, *Afghanistan: A Political History*, vol. 1 (Peshawar: privately published, 2002), 64–77.

common in the contemporary conflict, which has witnessed frequently shifting front lines and vacillating power structures in many areas of Afghanistan. This traditional practice calls on the known tribal elders of the area to approach the advancing army of the victorious power while ritually bearing a copy of the Koran and to give guarantees of good behavior on behalf of the defeated fighters. The value of the elders is that they embody social authority and have a pedigree known to both sides. Their guarantee that the fighters have pledged to cease hostilities is generally accepted. In turn, the victorious power responds by demanding that the fighters hand over their weapons and, especially in the case of victory by the state, any government property that they might have with them. The victor then pledges not to undertake any hostile act against those who are capitulating. As a token of good faith, the winning side—such as the state, after having reasserted its power—may even return some of the weapons or a vehicle for the protection of those who reconciled.

Depending on how the victor receives the approaches, the final outcome may be subjugation (the former combatants go home on parole) or co-option (the former combatants are integrated into the victorious army or its new administration). In 2001, many defeated Taliban invoked this form of reconciliation, handing in weapons and official assets to the Northern Alliance or pro-Karzai commanders and returning to their villages hoping to be able to reintegrate. For example, Mohammad Raheem Ishaqzai, a senior aide to Taliban civilian aviation minister Akhtar Mohammad Mansoor, initially handed over his weapons to Ishaqzai elders in Nauzad, Helmand. Only later, when the insurgency started, did he become Taliban (shadow) governor of the province. In Baghlan province, the Taliban administration had been largely dependent on local Hezb-i-Islami (Islamic Party) commanders. In 2001 and 2002, most of them agreed to terms directly with the Jamiat-i-Islami (Islamic Society) commanders who were empowered by the new administration; several later reemerged in public life as mid-ranking government officials. The availability of such traditional mechanisms means that combatants can make an exit from the conflict with some dignity. This traditional form of subjugation and co-option has been frequently used since the Soviet intervention and has contributed significantly to conflict management and to rapid stabilization after a main conflict has been settled.

Both *tiga* and the pledging of allegiance depend upon the role of tribal elders. A traditional reconciliation broker is designated a *salis ul khair*. He is someone accepted as a neutral and fair figure by both sides and is often a *syed* (a claimed descendant of the Prophet Mohammad), a senior religious scholar, or a distinguished tribal elder. The *salis* engages with both sides to a dispute and tries to reconcile them through a compromise. The institution of *jirga* may be used alongside or in place of the *salis*—with multiple variations in composition and authority. Any deal concluded by a *salis* or a *jirga* could be ritualized and guaranteed through the use of traditional instruments, such as *nagha* (fine), *machalgo* (surety), *yarghamal* (hostage), or *swara* (political marriage).

The experience of the Afghan tribes with the British in one hundred years of frontier politics and warfare, in which the conflicting parties built relationships on political agreements, is replete with references to traditional concepts such as *nagha* to manage conflict.[2] Through the nineteenth century and the first half of the twentieth century, the British colonial authorities in India sought to secure their Indian possessions from the northwest. The two major British military incursions into Afghanistan produced disastrous consequences for both sides, but the closed frontier strategy, whereby the British conducted political relations with Afghan tribes along the strip now known as Pakistan's Federally Administered Tribal Areas (FATA) and adjoining frontier territories, proved relatively successful. During this period, the tribes and the colonial authorities conducted multiple agreements. The standard formula invoked collective responsibility (in which elders gave undertakings for the behavior of their tribesmen) and territorial responsibility (in which elders gave undertakings on what would happen in their areas). In return, the tribes received guarantees of internal autonomy and incentives, such as subsidies or trade access.

To guarantee agreements, hostages were often pledged and force was used in the form of collective punishment. With regard to the terms of

---

2. Fida Yunas and Sher Zaman Taizi, eds., *Treaties, Engagements, and Sanads Relating to the North West Frontier Province* (Peshawar: Area Study Centre, Peshawar University, 2006.) This volume includes a selection of documents originally compiled by Sir C.U. Aitchison, published in 1929–1933.

the bargain, the frontier agreements generally constituted accommodations. Although the colonial authorities typically deployed sufficient force to negotiate from a position of strength, the agreements all offered the tribal parties some privileges and guarantees, especially safeguards for the autonomy of the tribe in its internal affairs. The practices fell well short of contemporary human rights norms. Indeed, in Pakistan, the Frontier Crimes Regulation, which incorporates many of the principles and practices of frontier politics, has been declared contrary to the fundamental rights otherwise provided for in the country's constitution. Nevertheless, the experience of the agreements in tribal and frontier areas offers the longest well-documented dataset of traditional Afghan institutions that have been used effectively in conflict management.

Reconciliation under the PDPA, 1978–1992

The best known reconciliation process from the era of the People's Democratic Party of Afghanistan (PDPA) rule was the United Nations-led mediation and Diego Cordovez's proximity talks, which ultimately led to the Geneva Accords and Soviet withdrawal. However, the PDPA also developed a broad repertoire of nonviolent approaches to the conflict and, along with massive injections of assistance, its pursuit of "national reconciliation" helped to prolong the life of the regime well beyond the Soviet withdrawal.

In terms of reconciliation initiatives directed by the intelligence domain, the PDPA-era Khad (Afghan intelligence service) was significantly more innovative and effective than the contemporary version. They established clandestine and semiclandestine links with the mujahideen armed opposition. Provincial intelligence directors were tasked with building up a relationship with all strategically important opposition commanders in their province. The Fifth Directorate (Antibanditism) specialized in exploiting these relationships. The work was structured with the use of protocols that the intelligence service entered into on behalf of the Afghan government and signed with opposition commanders or tribal elders in opposition-dominated areas. The protocols were supposedly secret, although often they were open secrets. The protocols amounted to nonaggression pacts, leaving the protocol commander in charge of security in a designated area and responsible for preventing hostile activities; in turn, the government provided financial and logistics support. The commanders superficially retained their armed opposition status but actually abstained from attacking government positions.

At the peak of the conflict in the mid-1980s, protocols were only marginally successful largely because mujahideen remained successful in mobilizing to fight the Soviet intervention. There were few takers and mujahideen were able to tactically exploit them. However, after the Soviet withdrawal, the protocols came into their own. In his latter years, Dr. Najibullah (Najib) and his regime successfully neutralized many of the opposition commanders who threatened government-held territory. For example, commanders of all seven main parties reached a modus vivendi with the regime around Kunduz town; on the approaches to Sarobi, the regime backed the Harakat-i-Inqilab commander to exclude Hezb-i-Islami; in Paghman, protocol commanders were used in conjunction with an expansion of the security perimeter; and in Behsud, a protocol neutralized the main Harakat-i-Islami commander. As commanders vied to benefit from relatively generous protocol terms, the Peshawar-based *tanzeem* (term used for the main politico-military groupings that fought the 1978–1992 jihad) leadership proved powerless to reverse the trend toward accommodation.

The most famous protocol of all was that signed between Ahmad Shah Masood's Shura Nizar and the Afghan government in 1984, providing for a truce in the Panjshir Valley. This truce provides a classic example of strategic exploitation of an agreement. Both sides agreed to the Panjshir protocol in response to war weariness, having suffered heavy casualties in offensives in the Panjshir Valley. The Afghan government and Soviets derived some benefit in terms of deflecting Masood away from the capital and protecting their supply line through the Salang Pass. However, Masood relied upon the Panjshir protocol to allow him to shift his focus to the northeast and to build up his Shura Nizar structure, which was crucial to his future war effort. Ultimately, an evaluation of the Panjshir protocol is complex. It failed the test of intentions, in that it is now clear that both sides were intent on returning to the conflict after availing of the strategic pause. But some of the relations established between figures in Masood's Shura Nizar and in the

PDPA in the wake of the Panjshir protocol proved to be long lasting, outliving the regime itself.

During this period, the regime also pursued a more transparent, political approach to wooing the armed opposition. The first significant political move for rapprochement made by the PDPA was the ten-point reconciliation program launched by Babrak Karmal in 1985, which was initiated upon Soviet advice and coincided with the rise of Mikhail Gorbachev to leadership of the Soviet Union.[3] The program was supposed to include the return of refugees, dialogue, political compromise, and a broadening of the base of the regime. However, little was done to operationalize Karmal's idea of national reconciliation. He was deposed six months later and it was left to his successor Najib to turn *ashti milli* (national reconciliation) into a more serious strategy. He announced his version in 1986, including a proposed cease-fire, a general amnesty, an invitation for the return of refugees, and a plan to form what was promised to be a broadly based government of national unity. The propagation of *ashti milli* became so high profile a component of Najib's political program that this particular phrasing of the idea of reconciliation has become irrevocably associated with the Najib era. Subsequent practitioners of reconciliation have been obliged to seek alternative official labels for what they seek to do as any program referring to *ashti milli* would inevitably be identified with the 1986 version.

To operationalize the strategy, the PDPA government launched a reconciliation commission to supervise the reintegration of mujahideen supporters who were prepared to accept the framework of law and government. The parallels with what has been tried under Hamid Karzai are remarkable. The original version of Najib's national reconciliation was based upon a subjugation-co-option model. Although it was backed by his international supporters who wanted to deescalate the conflict, it encountered significant resistance from regime insiders who were worried about diluting privileges. The reconciliation process was also launched in the wake of years of hostile official propaganda against the mujahideen, in conditions where regime partisans sought to protect their position by continuing to demonize and exclude the mujahideen.

---

3. Henry S. Bradsher, *Afghan Communism and Soviet Intervention* (Oxford: Oxford University Press, 1999), 145.

The early days of national reconciliation were thus accompanied by contradictory messages of enduring hostility toward the same mujahideen who were supposedly being wooed. While the Soviets still had troops in the country, national reconciliation had few high-level takers from the mujahideen ranks.

Despite the initial resistance from insiders and reluctance from mujahideen, the Najibullah regime pursued national reconciliation relentlessly. It was backed up by local diplomacy whereby administration and intelligence officials actively engaged with tribal leadership and commanders in the provinces, seeking deals that amounted to nonaggression pacts with the mujahideen that could be presented as national reconciliation. And it was paralleled by the covert work on protocols by the intelligence service. By 1987 Najib claimed to be shifting his national reconciliation from the original subjugation-co-option model to an accommodation approach, as he announced a political plan to incorporate the opposition into the regime. Notwithstanding mujahideen leadership rejection of every offer made, once the Soviet withdrawal went ahead, national reconciliation and the process of entering into protocols with the local opposition seemed to have had an impact on the ground. The government was increasingly successful in neutralizing armed actions and won the covert or overt cooperation of sufficient commanders to achieve some impact on the precarious security situation.

Despite the widespread expectation that the Najibullah regime would collapse rapidly after the completion of the Soviet withdrawal in February 1989, it struggled on for another three years until it was toppled in a militia revolt. National reconciliation and the accompanying instruments for engagement with the opposition should be recognized as contributory factors in the regime's ability to stave off defeat longer than expected. With the main casus belli of the Soviet presence removed, national reconciliation made it increasingly difficult for mujahideen commanders to sustain the conflict.

As the most consistently pursued reconciliation process during the Afghan conflict, the Najib-era national reconciliation program has left an enduring legacy. The post-2001 administration would borrow some of the instruments and even veteran personnel from the Najib-era program. However, it gave its own program for reaching out to the

Taliban a name that avoided use of the old key words that would have given the impression that a new government was simply dusting off Najib's old policies.

Some of the tools employed by Najib in the process of reconciling commander networks would most likely offend contemporary sensitivities. The regime typically lavished local currency on those who entered protocols and distributed significant quantities of small arms to them. In a remarkable turnaround, Najib's distribution of weapons to the opposition had more success in securing the regime than initial efforts to arm government supporters, the early militias. However, the price was paid in later insecurity, as factionalization of the mujahideen and small-arms proliferation contributed to the civil conflict. In the contemporary context—in the presence of a well-resourced international aid operation—there is ample scope to provide reconciling commander networks access to patronage through involvement in civilian projects or institutionalized security forces.

But why did Najib's reconciliation strategy achieve some strategic benefits when the earlier PDPA attempts did not? Upon taking over power, Hafizullah Amin, the second PDPA ruler, announced prisoner releases and a partial amnesty, employed some conciliatory rhetoric, and presided over an increase in the use of Islamic references and symbols in the official media. Similarly, when Karmal took over as leader, he largely emptied the main Pul-i-Charki prison of political prisoners. He was conciliatory in his early rhetoric and talked of broadening the base of government by inducting national figures who had stayed apart from it. Even so, it has never been seriously suggested that either Amin's flirt with a conciliatory approach or Karmal's early gestures achieved any impact on the conflict. In the first place, they were gestures rather than developed strategies and they were directly contradicted by the regime's main efforts. The irony of Amin's limited prisoner releases was that he continued and intensified the arrests, torture, and executions that characterized the early period of PDPA rule.

Although Karmal did not initially engage in the same kind of state repression that Nur Mohammad Taraki and Amin had presided over, the Soviet military intervention that brought him to power was so unpopular that it rendered conciliatory gestures largely irrelevant. The underlying political and military dynamics were beyond the capacity of the regime to manage, whether through national reconciliation or any other strategy. The situation proved irretrievable, and from the start the regime enjoyed minimal legitimacy. Rather than rallying the regime, the Soviet military intervention helped to mobilize resistance to it. The support for the mujahideen forces, particularly through Pakistan, was robust and the mujahideen were successful in militarily dominating much of the countryside and pinning the regime down to urban centers.

If Najibullah's national reconciliation was more successful than any of its predecessors and achieved some strategic impact after 1989, it was largely because of Soviet withdrawal and because the government forces proved more militarily robust than had been predicted. This created conditions in which a united reconciliation strategy was able to make significant progress in undermining mujahideen willingness and ability to fight. However, the lesson must also not be lost that Najib was ultimately unsuccessful in achieving a comprehensive political settlement, despite many efforts. The national reconciliation strategy became a process for warding off defeat rather than winning the war. In the end, reconciliation could not prop up a regime with doubtful domestic legitimacy and waning international backing.

Reconciliation under the Mujahideen and Taliban, 1992–2001

Top-level peacemaking attempts in the period after the collapse of the PDPA regime tell a tale of successive failures by international, regional, and Afghan actors to broker lasting deals among the warring parties. The efforts have been much documented and the failure of peacemaking initiatives among the mujahideen famously created the conditions in which the Taliban were able to grab power. The series of accords that failed to end the conflict included the Peshawar Accord of April 1992, which was an agreement on the first mujahideen government to be led first by Sebghatullah Mojadedi and then by Burhanuddin Rabbani; the Islamabad Accord of March 1993, which was an agreement on the terms of power sharing between Rabbani and Gulbadin Hekmatyar; and the Mahiper Accord of May 1995, which was an agreement on bringing Hekmatyar back into Rabbani's government. Each of these accords also included a political agreement on distribution of power in the central government as the centerpiece of what was supposed to be a comprehensive end to the fighting. The terms were accommodation-oriented, with the main parties accepting a stake in power.

Although the United Nations persisted with mediation tracks through the mujahideen and Taliban periods (1992–2001), and the secretary-general appointed a succession of envoys (Mahmoud Mistiri, Norbert Holl, Lakhdar Brahimi, and Francesc Vendrell), it had no major role in the accords that were signed. The international role in the failed rapprochement consisted of Pakistan hosting the accords, Saudi Arabia blessing them, and the United Nations watching them fall apart. External political or security mechanisms were not developed or deployed to support the intra-Afghan accords of this era. Whether the processes that lead to the successive failed accords of the 1990s should even merit consideration in discussions of current attempts at reconciliation is debatable. However, the opportunistic behavior of the factional leaders during the negotiation and implementation phases and the resulting failure of the accords to check the fighting are frequently condemned in Afghan commentary on the period. This in itself provides a strong incentive for the sponsors of any contemporary reconciliation effort to ensure that it is designed in such a way as to avoid any evocation of the failures of the 1990s.

Although less well known than the failed national-level political accords of the 1990s, there are multiple examples of indigenous reconciliation that occurred on various fronts during both the mujahideen and Taliban periods. Although none of these processes purported to directly transform the national-level conflict, they were used by parties to the conflict to rebuild and pursue their war objectives through political means. They constitute further examples of how even in times of war Afghan statecraft draws on reconciliation traditions.

While the Taliban are mainly remembered for an uncompromising stance, often humiliating and executing their defeated opponents, they too employed some reconciliation tools. From their campaign in the east, for instance, there are examples of political accommodation, such as in Laghman province's Gonapal Valley. This remote, forested valley was one of Afghanistan's anomalies, having maintained a self-declared autonomous administration, complete with self-styled "prime minister" and "cabinet." The Taliban eventually entered the valley in force and captured the self-declared leadership. However, Mawlvi Kabeer signed an agreement with the Gonapal leadership on terms that clearly amounted to accommodation, whereby he acknowledged (or perhaps humored) the valley leaders, left them in charge of local security, and awarded them a cash subsidy in return for declaring loyalty to the Islamic Emirate of Afghanistan. Similarly, in contrast to the uncompromising stance in the southwest, the Taliban sent an intermediary to senior Hezb-i-Islami commander Engineer Qarar of Laghman. He too accepted a cash subsidy and agreed to cease hostilities against the Islamic Emirate. A senior Taliban leader who served as governor in the north described to the author how his favorite achievement was to have reached an accommodation with local commanders in Jowzjan province, which allowed him to transfer a district administration to them.

In Hazarajat, the Taliban were acutely aware of the challenge of subduing an area where they had no prior alliances and no known natural supporters. After a successful military campaign in which they militarily routed the Hezb-i-Wahadat defenders, the Taliban pursued a diplomacy that amounted to reconciliation. In the first place, they identified the top political leader-cum-commander who had stayed in the area, Ustad Akbari. They selected appropriate envoys and made a successful approach to him. Although Ustad Akbari never accepted an official position in the Taliban administration, he played a crucial role in helping them to establish that administration and in stabilizing the region until the military tide turned again.

There are more local examples from Hazarajat of Taliban deal making. In the first winter of Taliban rule in Hazarajat (1998–99), for example, the mujahideen of Shahristan rebelled, captured the Taliban contingent in their district, expelled them, and took control of the district. The following spring, rather than adopting a purely military approach, which could have involved fighting with a long and vulnerable communications line, the Taliban sent Ustad Akbari along with the top Taliban military commander in the region to seek a negotiated outcome. They reached an accommodation, which proved to be relatively long lasting, whereby the Shahristan mujahideen recognized the supremacy of the Islamic Emirate and supplied a hundred conscripts for service outside the district as a token of this recognition. But as part of the deal, the Shahristan mujahideen were allowed to run a largely autonomous administration with a Hazara district administrator, no external-force presence, and no compulsion to implement any of the infamous Taliban social policies. One result of this was that girls' education continued in Shahristan without interruption throughout the Taliban period—all funded by local taxes. As these examples demonstrate, even the most ruthless of recent Afghan factions has included engagement with the enemy and appropriate reconciliation instruments in their campaign portfolio.

Reconciliation under the Bonn Architecture, 2001–2005

Some of the most tangible progress toward reconciliation after the Bonn Accords occurred not in the context of dedicated reconciliation programs but as a consequence of belligerents availing of opportunities to participate in the political process. Most criticism of the Bonn Accords has focused on one particular shortcoming of the process—specifically, how power in the post-Taliban administration was allocated between one belligerent party, the Northern Alliance, and those Afghan émigré groups who had no armed presence in Afghanistan but who had previously participated in a structured dialogue with the United Nations (the Rome, Cyprus, and Peshawar groups). While most past criticism of the accords focused on the underrepresentation of politically important Pashtoons in the process, most recent criticism has suggested that Taliban participation in Bonn and in the new administration might have helped to forestall the subsequent insurgency. In interpreting Bonn, however, it is important to track the ways in which some figures associated with the Taliban regime did manage to join the new system—despite the Taliban's absence from the Bonn conference.

Although Bonn was not a peace agreement, the architecture of the agreement left space for a reconciliation element in the subsequent political process. The accords prepared the way for a broadening of the base of the regime to mitigate the problem of the initial concentration of power. The key political processes that provided opportunities for erstwhile opposition figures to legitimize themselves as members of the new political order included the Loya Jirga (Grand Council) and the elections to the Parliament and provincial councils. The regulations adopted for these processes were relatively free of any catch-all exclusions for those formerly associated with the Taliban. As a result, a number of mid-level and senior figures from the Taliban administration availed of the opportunity provided by the Loya Jirga. They presented themselves as candidates in the indirect elections and, where they could mobilize some popular support, they joined the *jirga*, thus claiming an "insider" status in post-Taliban Afghanistan. This process continued in the parliamentary and provincial elections, where a number of prominent figures who had been associated with the Taliban regime presented themselves as candidates and found their way into the lower and upper houses.

Many of the former combatants who took this route were individuals who had a political identity other than their Taliban identity, often a predating one. Generally speaking, they were commanders who had first achieved prominence as mujahideen within the main jihadi parties and who had after 1994 allied themselves with the Taliban and served the Taliban only as long as the movement remained the dominant force. Many of the peers of these temporary Taliban were already in the administration or its security forces. They used the Loya Jirga and elections as part of the process of reasserting their old identities, ensuring that they were rehabilitated in the new order without any stigma from their period with the Taliban. Even so, the parliamentary elections also illustrated the difficulty of an electoral road in reconciling or rehabilitating core Taliban. Those who did stand for election found it difficult to mobilize the popular vote. In the southwest, for example, voting patterns were largely tribal. The Taliban either found that they belonged to tribes whose vote blocks were too small to win seats (Wakil Ahmad Mutawakil) or that they could not win the backing of their own tribe (Mullah Khaksar). As a result, the few core Taliban candidates in the parliamentary elections either withdrew in favor of stronger tribal candidates or were resoundingly defeated.

2

The Post-2001 Conflict

It is axiomatic that any effective reconciliation strategy must be based on a firm understanding of the conflict to which it is being applied. Analysis of the Afghan insurgency as it has developed since the international intervention in autumn 2001 provides some useful insights into the country's possible reconciliation options. Indeed, one cannot understand the present full-fledged insurgency against the Afghan government without first briefly examining the principal transitional phases of the conflict that Afghanistan has witnessed since 2001.

The first transitional phase of the post-2001 conflict was strikingly brief. Coalition attacks on the Taliban began on October 7, 2001, leading up to the Northern Alliance taking over Kabul on November 13 and the Taliban surrendering their last major center, Kandahar, on December 7. The last large-scale battle of the war to displace the Taliban, fought between the coalition and remnants of the Taliban–al-Qaida military, was Operation Anaconda in Paktia in March 2002. In May 2003, U.S. defense secretary Donald Rumsfeld announced that major U.S. combat operations in Afghanistan had ended—ironically, when this announcement was made, the ground had already been laid for the Taliban to launch its insurgency.

Although some fighting continued, the second transitional phase—the post-conflict lull—effectively began in December 2001 and lasted throughout 2002. After the Taliban lost its last administrative center, the interim administration installed through the Bonn Accords was recognized across the country as the successor regime, and the succession was not contested. Tribal delegations from all provinces pledged allegiance to the new administration, either contacting the rapidly appointed provincial governors or traveling to Kabul to present their compliments. Although UN representative Lakhdar Brahimi reiterated in July 2002 that the Taliban and al-Qaida remained a threat to security in Afghanistan, there was no serious insurgent violence in 2002. Despite dire warnings to the contrary, the Taliban did not disrupt the Loya Jirga held in June 2002. Indeed, members of the commission organizing the Loya

Jirga were able to travel freely throughout Afghanistan with no security in the months leading up to the event.

The third transitional stage of the post-2001 conflict began in January 2003 and was first marked by a significant pitched battle between coalition soldiers and a force of some eighty Taliban. This battle was followed by a series of attacks on aid workers, including a most disturbing summary execution of an International Committee of the Red Cross (ICRC) expatriate worker, apparently upon direct orders of Taliban commander Dadaullah. Although insurgent violence remained relatively low and sporadic in 2003, the growing insurgency started to limit humanitarian efforts, prompting a cessation of United Nations missions to Kandahar and Helmand provinces. Throughout 2004, insurgents continued with their established pattern of executing sporadic raids and rocket attacks. Even so, they did attempt their first targeted escalation of the violence by mounting a series of attacks on the presidential election process. But in the end, their violence was not on a sufficient scale to disrupt the election. Even in 2005, it was still possible to drive the main Kabul-Kandahar highway in relative confidence.

The first major escalation in the insurgency began in 2006, when a suicide bombing campaign led to the death of a top Canadian diplomat, and the Taliban adopted the IED (improvised explosive device) as a preferred method of ambush. The commander networks associated with the original Taliban movement remobilized in provinces inhabited by the Kandahari tribes—Kandahar, Helmand, Urozgan, Zabul, and Farah. In the southeast, local commanders loyal to older mujahideen networks emerged in the Loya Paktia provinces of Khost, Paktia, and Paktika and in Ghazni. Although many of these commanders depended on an operating base in Waziristan, they were able to mobilize fighters who lived in the southeastern provinces. Over time, Jalaluddin Haqani and his clan emerged as the most effective mobilizers of commanders in this region.

The largest province in the east, Nangarhar, stayed remarkably peaceful, but armed groups mobilized in Kunar, either mounting hit-and-run operations across the border from Bajaur Agency or establishing themselves in resistance pockets where they had significant local support, such as in the troubled Korangal Valley. Although not directly related to the insurgency, riots in Kabul in May 2006 symbolized a collapse in confidence in the ability of the government to provide security.

Through 2007, the Taliban continued with their attacks in the core provinces of the insurgency and expanded into new areas, including the provinces adjoining Kabul and the provinces in the northwest with a significant Pashtoon minority. By the spring of 2008, with the insurgency escalating further still in intensity, the Taliban had succeeded in plunging a third of the country back into full-scale conflict. By that point, the campaign that they had sustained was longer than the one that they had waged to conquer most of Afghanistan in 1994–1998.

The Insurgency's Effect on Reconciliation Strategy

In the first half of 2002, it was not inevitable that the Taliban would choose to mount an insurgency. Even Hamid Karzai publicly left the door open to the possibility of the Taliban playing a role in government. Indeed, in the first few months of 2002, there were examples of positive, high-level contacts between interim officials and members of the movement's leadership. Even so, the lull between the collapse of the Taliban administration and the launch of the insurgency was not a period of total peace and tranquility. The main visible threat to Afghan security throughout 2002 and into 2003 was a series of local clashes between nominally progovernment forces who were vying for shares of power and influence in the new setup.

In the first six months of 2002—the period of the interim administration—twelve serious armed conflicts took place in different regions of the country. Forces operating under the Ministry of Defense were involved in all of these conflicts, and in most of these conflicts both sides were affiliated with the ministry. This was not an insurgency but a resurgence of the long-running factional conflict in which local parties were vying for both control on the ground and recognition by the government. The process of the new administration asserting its authority over its own allies was messy and protracted and created the impression that the warlords (southern and northern) against whom the Taliban had rebelled in 1994 were going to have the upper hand in the new regime. This provided a powerful incentive for the Taliban to hold back from the new administration and to prepare for a resumption of the struggle.

Much has been written about the flight of Taliban leaders to Pakistan in late 2001. However, the majority of Taliban, including some leaders, opted to stay in Afghanistan. They invoked the traditional mechanisms for recognizing the new authority and tried to reintegrate into the new political reality. For many, this meant simply going home. But most were left in an ambiguous position in terms of their status relative to the new administration and coalition forces. Even before the international intervention, the UN Security Council had maintained a list of sanctioned individuals, Taliban leaders, and senior officials, although it was not a "wanted list" per se, as sanctions did not confer any powers of arrest. The United States, meanwhile, had separately developed a "blacklist" of figures suspected of involvement in terrorism whom it wanted to detain. This list had significant overlap with the UN sanctions list but included more Taliban military commanders and figures suspected of assisting al-Qaida.

One theme of the politics of the interim and transitional administrations during the 2002–04 period was the debate over the merits and composition of "blacklists" of former regime officials wanted for questioning. Those favoring an inclusive approach and rapid moves to reconciliation argued for a minimalist approach to the compilation of any blacklist. Those who believed that there was an immediate terrorist threat or who sought factional advantage argued for long blacklists. But even the longest blacklist compiled at the national level (for example, as advocated by Marshall Faheem, who advocated a list of 150 names) did not affect the majority of former officials and personnel. Although the new administration made no legal moves against those on the list, they were vulnerable to the initiative of local security officials who, irrespective of the lack of specific legal grounds, could arrest them arbitrarily or implicate them in the harboring of al-Qaida fugitives ("Arabs"). It was to ward off this threat of arbitrary and usually predatory action that former Taliban invoked the traditional reconciliation mechanisms, pledging allegiance to and claiming the protection of approachable figures in the new administration.

The coalition had a very thin presence on the ground initially and was highly dependent on local collaborators and the revived Afghan

National Directorate of Security (NDS) for identification of "the enemy." There was a widespread perception among Afghans in the first couple of years of the intervention that Afghan translators working with coalition forces often manipulated the flow of information to their employers to direct them toward fellow Afghans with whom they were involved in personal feuds rather than toward those who posed a real threat to the administration or coalition forces.

As an example of how the Taliban successfully utilized network links to the new authorities, a Taliban deputy minister from Kandahar belonging to the Ishaqzai tribe was able to invoke his tribal identity to avoid arrest. His father was a known elder of the tribe who had long participated in tribal *jirgas* at the provincial level. On this basis, father and son approached the new provincial governor, Gul Agha Sherzai, a Barakzai. The Barakzai and Ishaqzai are both important Pashtoon tribes in Kandahar. Although Gul Agha Sherzai's principal reputation is as a commander and not as a tribal leader, the deputy minister was able to assert his tribal identity and invoke the fact that their fathers had long interacted in tribal dealings. As a result, Gul Agha gave the deputy minister his personal assurance that he would be allowed to resume a normal life and even establish a business in Kandahar city.

Despite this example, however, there are multiple counterexamples of how those who had been associated with the Taliban regime were prevented from making such a peaceful transition, with some ultimately actively participating in the insurgency. For example, Haji Mateen, who was not an official in the Taliban regime but who was in Kunar during the Taliban period and had been associated with the Salafi movement in the province, claims that after the fall of the Taliban he went to live peacefully in his home in the district center Manogai. But factional rivals triggered a coalition forces raid on his house, demonstrating to him that his honor and status could not be safeguarded in the new dispensation. As a result, he joined the insurgent front in Korangal.

In the old Taliban heartland of the southwestern provinces in particular, the administrations appointed by the new government adopted highly predatory tactics. Despite attempts by former Taliban to reintegrate, the administrations launched a campaign against known adherents of the deposed regime, subjecting them to arbitrary arrest, seizure of vehicles and other assets, and general harassment. During 2002, second-tier Taliban leaders were driven underground and across the border into Pakistan. A key feature of the chronology of the regrouping of just about every Taliban network is the tale of how their commanders were driven out of southern Afghanistan before they launched the insurgency—not after.

Characteristics of the Insurgency

The apparent lack of political developments in the insurgency has been remarkable. The composition of the Taliban-Kandahar insurgency is little changed from the early days, except for the loss of senior figures who have been killed or arrested. Apart from the mobilization of the Haqani network and the smaller networks in the east and the return of Hezb-i-Islami leader Hekmatyar to the fray, there has been little notable movement into or out of the insurgency by major Afghan figures and little recruitment or defection. Those political developments that have occurred have much more to do with the international composition of the insurgency, in particular the reorganization of al-Qaida, the mobilization of Pakistani jihadi groups, and the emergence of the Pakistani Tehreek-i-Taliban.

One politically significant post-2001 development in the Taliban modus operandi has been the development of relatively sophisticated media operations. Ustad Yasser, formerly an aide to government ally Abdul Rab Sayyaf, is one of the few nationally known mujahideen figures who, since 2001, has sided with the Taliban. That he has been active as a Taliban propagandist, contributing to the refashioning of the Taliban media profile, illustrates how much worse the insurgency could be if the Taliban were able to attract and retain influential supporters. To date, however, the insurgency has been remarkably passive politically speaking. The post-2001 insurgency has not been guided by any modern political movement and does not represent an identifiable set of interest groups or manifest a clear structure with an articulated political agenda.

The insurgency is composed of a conglomeration of different networks that are sometimes referred to for convenience as "the Taliban." But in reality the insurgents do not belong to any single coherent organization. Although they might frequently strive to project an image of unity, referring to themselves as Taliban or even invoking the name of supreme leader Mullah Omar and participating in joint *shuras* (consultations), the insurgents do not all "belong" to Mullah Omar's Tehreek-i-Taliban. Rather, insurgents "belong" to what might be described as commander-solidarity networks. The networks are based upon comradeship, a shared background and common outlook, and patronage links with the key commander figures in the network. Commanders within the insurgency depend upon the solidarity within their own networks to mobilize men and command their loyalty. The lowest common denominator among the networks seems to be opposition to Karzai and his Western backers, a willingness to wage violent jihad, and a propensity to espouse the cause of establishing an Islamic system.

The nearest thing to a "membership" process in the insurgency is the use of *bayat* (pledge of loyalty). Specifically, commanders wanting to associate themselves with the Taliban pledge loyalty to Mullah Omar. Despite such pledges, the networks around the top Taliban commanders of Kandahar, the networks around Mawlvi Jalaluddin Haqani and Latif Mansoor in the southeast, the supporters of the late Mawlvi Khalis in the east, and the Salafist networks in Kunar are in actuality all discrete entities. Each network mobilizes and supplies its own men, operates in its own areas where it draws upon its own relationships with the tribes and administration, and discreetly develops its own operating practices. In short, each of these networks is only dependent on a modicum of cooperation with other parts of the insurgency.

The role of the commander-solidarity networks explains much of the robustness of the insurgency despite the massive effort and resources directed toward the Kabul administration and counterinsurgency. Within a part of the Afghan social milieu, each of these networks commands legitimacy, trust, and loyalty and has built up its capabilities on them. Despite all the reverses and casualties suffered by the Taliban, many Afghans still find these commander networks sufficiently familiar, accessible, and reliable to entrust themselves or their sons to them. These same Afghans tend to find most state institutions remote, hostile, unreliable, and ultimately illegitimate. One of the key dilemmas of Western intervention in Afghanistan is that the internationals' points of contact for their strategically important business are predominantly within the formal institutions, such as the administration, police, and army. These institutions all have structural limitations on what they can achieve in an environment where all the real Afghan business is conducted through informal networks. The importance of the commander-solidarity networks in sustaining the conflict and the limitations of the formal state institutions in countering the networks both have to be addressed in designing approaches to reconciliation.

Because of the existence of the multiple networks within the insurgency, it is difficult to characterize the specific outlook of the leadership—this varies among the networks. For example, unlike other networks, the Kandahari Taliban leaders could perhaps be described as stubborn and more rhetorical than ideological and capable of displaying pragmatism when it suits them. Furthermore, they are often much more tactically focused than strategically focused and are concerned more about their requirements of cash and materiel and their calls for prisoner releases than about the future of Afghanistan. The commander networks in eastern Afghanistan operate in an entirely different tribal milieu from the Kandahari tribes, and some of them tend to be much more clearly focused on rivalries left over from the jihad and factional conflict periods. Their rivals from that era have received dominant positions in the administration and security forces. As a result, the commanders have sought patronage in the insurgency to fight back. Each network has a distinctive political calculus. One common key aspect of the insurgent leadership, however, is that most of the top commanders tend to spend extended periods in Pakistan and seem little inclined to travel within Afghanistan.

During the Taliban period of rule, there was generally a blurring of the distinction between combatant and civilian, with civilian officials often taking time off to spend time at the front. In the last year of their rule, the Taliban maintained between forty and forty-five thousand men under arms. Each commander had a *tashkeel*, which consisted of an authorized number of men attached to a designated military unit, for which he could claim a ration allowance (*ayasha*) either from the front to which they were deployed or from the Ministry of Defense. In reality, there was a high turnover and circulation of the personnel within these *tashkeel*s, as commanders drew men from their solidarity networks or from tribes that had pledged conscripts.[1]

After 2001, as the movement readjusted itself, a new dynamic emerged between the civilian and military realms. The number of individuals actively involved in the fighting is now lower than in the Taliban's heyday, but the number of hangers-on has not diminished. This is because for many people being associated with the Taliban is indeed about belonging to a network as opposed to actively participating in an armed struggle. They maintain their links to senior comrades in the insurgency as a way of maintaining social relations, from which they benefit in multiple ways. The most obvious is in maintaining a claim on resources. Indeed, Taliban comrades can claim a share of the resources commanded by the various fronts, even without being too active in the fighting. In developing strategies to address the conflict, it is important to acknowledge the importance of the insurgency to livelihood. An invitation to reconciliation that is also an invitation to abandon one's livelihood may be less than convincing, particularly in the absence of an alternative.

The insurgents are predominantly Pashtoon, drawn from almost all the Pashtoon tribes. In some places there is a local logic to which tribe features most prominently in the insurgency. Whichever tribe is the outsider in the local power struggle generally tends to supply more men to the insurgency. Although some of the insurgents are mobile and engage in operations far from their home area, the insurgents usually operate locally. That is, they operate in areas where their tribe has a presence. Thus, most of the insurgents operating in the greater Kandahar zone of the southwest are from the Kandahari tribes, while most of those operating in the east are from the eastern tribes. Within this pattern of local roots, the northern Pashtoons play a significant role. Significant numbers of Taliban operating in the southwest are men from Kandahari tribes whose clans had historically settled in the north but who were displaced during the war. They have also helped the insurgents launch activities in the north.

---

1. Anthony Davis, "Foreign Fighters Step Up Activity in Afghan Civil War," *Jane's Intelligence Review* 13, no. 8 (August 1, 2001).

In terms of the insurgency's leadership, the top echelon is composed of commanders who came to prominence during the Taliban's rise and period in government. There has been remarkably little "fresh blood" in terms of newly emerging top leaders, even though significant numbers of leaders and top commanders have been killed or captured. The mid-level of the command structure is composed of commanders from the Taliban campaigns of the 1990s, some of whom command smaller units now than in their heyday (largely because the insurgent army is smaller than the one the Taliban had previously mobilized). It is also composed of combatants who have been recently promoted to commander, providing some "new blood." Many of these recently promoted local commanders were either too young to command during the Taliban heyday or were simply not affiliated with the organization in the past.

Most of the component networks in the insurgency have well-developed links to Pakistan. For example, many have dwellings, supporters, affiliated madrassahs, and well-developed social networks in Baluchistan, the North-West Frontier Province (NWFP), FATA, or the cities of Sindh and Punjab. These links have been developed over three decades. The Kandahari tribes sssentially treat Pakistan's Baluchistan as part of their social and economic space. Their business activities and labor migration patterns flow across southwestern Afghanistan and western Pakistan (often also taking in the rest of Afghanistan and the Middle East), with little regard to the border. Their insurgency has followed the same sociogeographical template. The eastern insurgents draw on similar economic and social links to Pakistan, especially in Peshawar.

In terms of social status, the mid- and low-level commanders and combatants are barely distinguishable from the rural population of the areas in which they are recruited and active. Although the commanders include a preponderance of young men who have studied in madrassahs, Taliban fighters tend to come from poor, conservative, rural backgrounds and tend to have little secular education and limited exposure to urban life or to the wider world beyond what they have seen in their local search for labor.

In terms of the insurgents' operating methods, most sections of the insurgency have developed ruthlessness as an in-house style, even more so now than pre-2001. In fact, the insurgents have developed a reputation for using extreme and arbitrary violence, including in internal disciplinary practices. This means that any insurgent engaged in unauthorized contacts with the enemy (or in reconciliation) faces the risk of execution.

In terms of the combatants' self-perception, the insurgents in general and Taliban in particular have a sense of themselves as being moral and noncorrupt. They generally consider themselves to be fighting a just cause and consider their forces to be disciplined and honest, in contrast to the government forces that they characterize as morally corrupt. For example, with regard to personal behavior, the institutional tradition of the Taliban movement includes bans on the smoking of cigarettes and hashish, partly in reaction to the way that these vices were popularized in the ranks of both mujahideen and government troops—which represented an outward manifestation of the moral decay of the forces that took part in the anti-Soviet jihad. In contrast, the Taliban are well-equipped with arguments to justify the cultivation and taxation of narcotics if they are consumed by non-Muslims (self-serving as these arguments may be). Although in practice they have demonstrated a high degree of solidarity in avoiding defections, there are, of course, important differences of outlook among insurgents, including some hierarchy-linked differences of interest. For example, unlike higher-level commanders, who have greater control of resources and are often able to remove themselves from the threat of physical danger, lower-level commanders must cope with meager resources and face relatively high mortality rates. As a result, they more readily express a willingness to reconcile.

The role of al-Qaida in the current phase of the conflict and the dynamics of the relationship between al-Qaida and the Afghan elements of the insurgency have strong implications for the prospects of reconciliation. The standard account of the Taliban's early relationship with al-Qaida is that Osama bin Laden, after his return to Afghanistan in 1996, successfully capitalized on the Taliban's isolation and need for resources in their civil war against the remnants of the mujahideen. Although al-Qaida remained organizationally separate from the Taliban, it exploited its alliance with the Afghan leadership primarily to win space to pursue its global jihad ambitions and secondarily to influence the development of the Taliban version of the Islamic state. Taliban leader Mullah Omar famously declined to break this alliance or surrender Osama bin Laden, even when faced with the prospect that continued protection of al-Qaida would render a U.S. intervention inevitable.

Despite its fugitive status after 2001, al-Qaida succeeded in relocating to Pakistan, where it reorganized and resumed its role of supplying manpower, technical expertise, and fundraising links to the Afghan insurgents. Developments in the insurgents' relationship with al-Qaida since 2001 have included a decentralization of the linkages. Whereas under the Islamic Emirate the relationship was centralized by the Taliban version of the state, today al-Qaida is able to relate to multiple Afghan fronts separately, often on the basis of jihad-era relationships (for example, with Jalaluddin Haqqani in the southeast) or ideological affinity (for example, with Salafi networks in the east). Even so, al-Qaida remains both peripheral and pivotal to the insurgency. It is peripheral in that its personnel—albeit revered—is alien to and excluded from the command of Afghan units. It is pivotal first in that access to finance is a key factor in sustaining the conflict, second in that the goals of Taliban and al-Qaida converge on demands for foreign troop withdrawal, and third in that Taliban leader Mullah Omar still seems committed to maintaining the alliance despite its obvious costs.

A common thread in Afghan government and international thinking on reconciliation has been that any arrangement would be between the Afghan parties and would exclude al-Qaida. Although some inside the original Taliban leadership are highly critical of al-Qaida's contribution to the perpetuation of conflict in Afghanistan, there has been no open move by any significant network in the insurgency to challenge the special relationship.

3

An Assessment of Post-2001 Reconciliation Efforts

Despite the recurrent interest in reconciliation, there has been little effort to date to assess the efficacy of the various reconciliation processes pursued since 2001. A theme common to the different processes is that they have tried to create conditions in which figures associated with the armed opposition could reintegrate peacefully and live in the territory controlled by the Afghan government. This reflects a minimalist conception of reconciliation in comparison to reconciliation processes elsewhere in the world that have aimed to restore relationships and create lasting peace. However, this conception of reconciliation offers a concrete means of measuring progress in terms of counting the number of politically or militarily significant figures associated with the armed opposition who have reintegrated peacefully, whether through formal processes or alternative routes.

As measured by this method, progress has been worryingly slow. To date, only 12 out of the 142 Taliban figures named in the UN Security Council sanctions list have reconciled and been reintegrated into public life in Afghanistan—or about 8 percent of "strategically significant" figures over a six-year period. Another ten Taliban leaders of equivalent rank not on the list have also reconciled. (For a list of those Taliban leaders who have reconciled, see appendix A.) Such figures give a better indication of the slowness of progress being made than the highly inflated figures of individuals entering the Proceayee Tahqeem Solha (Strengthening Peace Program, or PTS). Under this officially endorsed scheme, former combatants who pledge to live peacefully receive a safe-conduct letter. By the end of 2007, the scheme claimed to have reconciled 4,634 former combatants. The UN list is the most transparent record of individuals who have been significant in the Taliban movement. It is reasonable to refer to it as a record of reconciliation progress because it provides a statement of all those who are considered senior in the movement and is not simply a selective "blacklist" of individuals to be arrested. The PTS figures cannot be relied on as an indicator of reconciliation progress because there is no record of the potential population from which they draw and against which progress might be measured. Furthermore, few individuals in the PTS caseload are of strategic significance, and criteria for entry into the program are so vague that potentially much of the population would be eligible.

Although reconciliation of senior Taliban is far more likely to impact on the insurgency than that of "foot soldiers," few senior figures have reconciled. Additionally, the few reconcilers who have been senior enough to have some impact on the conflict have mostly brokered their deals with the administration through their own informal channels and not through the formal reconciliation program. In any case, most politically significant reconcilers made their move before the escalation in the insurgency; the flow of senior figures toward reconciliation has since largely dried up. All of this belies the official claims that large numbers of important insurgents have reconciled. Analysis of the twenty-two significant figures who have reconciled indicates the following:

- The majority of the senior Taliban who have reconciled have done so through a process best described as "political sponsorship" (12 out of 22).
- Direct intervention by the executive has played a significant role in the reconciliation of senior Taliban (8 out of 22).
- The PTS was the primary contact for the leaders in only one case. Although leaders were processed through PTS in several other cases, they made their political deal with another part of the administration.
- Release from detention has also been a significant route into reconciliation, with five high-profile detainees reconciling through that route; all of them were helped by the active involvement of the executive.
- Most of the reconciled leaders played primarily a civilian rather than military role under the Taliban (15 out of 22).
- The vast majority of those leaders who have reconciled played no role in the post-2001 insurgency (19 out of 22).
- Those reconciled leaders who had been active in the post-2001 insurgency depended upon the president personally directing the

National Security Council (NSC) and Western allies to arrange their reconciliation.

- Affiliation to networks other than the Taliban seems to have been a significant factor in reconciliation; one reconciled leader had been affiliated with Zahir Shah, and 8 out of 22 had been known as mujahideen commanders before their spell with the Taliban.
- There has been almost no reconciliation of top-level leaders since the escalation of the insurgency from 2005 onward.

Most reconciling Taliban have sought the protection and support of a senior figure in the administration, based on an old acquaintance or network links. This is what has been referred to as "political sponsorship." The reliance of Taliban leaders on such an informal process to make their transition into the new setup is entirely consistent with tradition and reflects the importance of patronage, networks, and alliances in the survival strategies of protagonists in Afghanistan's conflict. It was epitomized by Musa Hotak, a Pashtoon commander with a long experience of interacting with the Hazaras. He had maintained discreet links with Hazara leader Ustad Khalili during the period of Khalili's anti-Taliban resistance. As the Taliban collapsed, Musa physically relocated to Khalili's camp.

The early figures to reconcile this way were those whose political identity was basically as mujahideen. Veterans such as Abdul Salaam Rocketi of Zabul and Mawlvi Arsala Rahmani of Paktika, who had earned their reputations in the era of jihad before siding with the Taliban, were able to present themselves as more *mujahid* than *talib*. Most of the leading figures in Karzai's administration based their reputation on having been mujahideen. Thus, the veterans were able to assert that they had credentials just as good as anyone else to be accepted into the new order.

Having held a top-level Taliban military command was apparently no barrier to reconciliation. For example, Abdul Salaam Rocketi was a Taliban corps commander in the eastern zone, but he was able to reassert his past mujahideen credentials and links to the Gailani family as early as September 2001 and eventually ended up in Parliament. As a sign of how much they had integrated into the new order, six of the reconciled leaders stood as candidates in the parliamentary election. (Mawlvi Islam, Musa Hotak, and Salaam Rocketi were all elected.) Some figures who eventually availed of political sponsorship in 2005 would have reconciled and reintegrated earlier if they had been given the slightest encouragement. The network of Taliban from Paktia and Paktika around Mawlvi Arsala Rahmani sat in Islamabad for almost three years, waiting for the Afghan government to clear their move to Kabul. They were eventually rewarded following Rahmani's promotion to the Senate.

Apart from the "drying up" of top-level reconciliation after 2005, the key issue of concern is that there has been a disconnect between the reconciliation process and the insurgency. Although reconciliation of Taliban leaders may have made some contribution to broadening the political base of the regime—and gave the regime the basis on which to claim that reconciliation is a workable option for those who were associated with the Taliban—the only three reconciled leaders who at some stage had any involvement in the insurgency were Abdul Wahid, Mullah Mujahid, and Abdul Salaam Rocketi. It appears that reconciliation has essentially not been pursued or delivered as an option for middle- or senior-level commanders, the figures who are most directly significant for stabilization. There is little evidence that any active middle- or senior-level insurgents have entered reconciliation through the PTS. After its formation in 2002, the Afghan National Security Council took on the task of collating the various blacklists prepared by the U.S. and Afghan security forces, with a focus on identifying figures implicated in the new insurgency. However, none of the commanders found on the NSC blacklists has availed of reconciliation. There is thus little evidence to suggest that reconciliation efforts have delivered any strategically significant contribution to managing the conflict.

4

The Politics of Reconciliation

The Afghan Taliban have so far refrained from establishing a civilian or political wing parallel to their military wing. They did not avail of the opportunities that were in principle available to them to encourage their representatives to participate in the Loya Jirga or parliamentary elections. However, this lack of structure does not mean that the Taliban can simply be dismissed as a fringe group—of no great political standing—that uses violence because of an absence of popular support. To understand the implications of the absence of Taliban participation in the new order, it is important to analyze the social and political standing of the movement.

In terms of their core identity, the Taliban comprise a movement of Afghans trained in and networked through the Deobandi madrassahs. The movement's core membership and most of the top leadership are drawn from the social circle of those who have stayed and studied in the madrassahs of greater Kandahar and Ghazni, or in the Afghan-linked parts of the Deobandi madrassah system in Pakistan.[1] When the movement was launched in 1994, Mullah Omar and his associates rapidly conducted a mobilization of cadres with common values and background by recruiting, in particular, from the NWFP and Baluchistan madrassahs. The movement has always considered itself supratribal, and Taliban veterans proudly and wistfully describe how in the heyday of the movement Taliban had little knowledge of one another's tribal identity. It is possible to establish empirically that the leadership was predominantly drawn from the Kandahar tribes, with a slight preponderance from the smaller and "weaker" tribes (such as Kakar or Ishaqzai) rather than the "dominant" tribes (such as the Barakzai or Alakozai). However, tribal identity was less important for the Taliban in the 1990s than today.

Although the top leadership circle came from a certain tribal milieu, the tribal base of the Taliban movement broadened even in its

---

1. Mariam Abou Zahab, *Islamist Networks: The Afghan-Pakistan Connection* (London: Hurst, 2004).

first year, as figures from the madrassah-based networks of the southeast and east of the country also joined them. This wave of recruits related to Mullah Omar as fellow Taliban and belonged to the same madrassah networks, but came from a different tribal milieu, the eastern tribes. Many of the 1994 recruits had no previous experience in politics and came fresh from their madrassahs. However, those who were veterans of the jihad had mainly been affiliated with Harakat-i-Inqilab or the faction of Hezb-i-Islami led by Younas Khalis. These two *tanzeem*s (organizations) had attracted most of the traditional mullahs who had fought in jihad. Their commanders and men, who were still organized as armed fronts that had fought the jihad and had their own links to peers in the mosques and madrassahs, constituted powerful networks. The Harakat-i-Inqilab and Hezb-i-Islami (Khalis) networks were rapidly absorbed in the movement. On the one hand, the ability of the new movement to recruit from the madrassahs and related networks gave it easy access to manpower. On the other hand, the movement's close association with the madrassahs meant that it could claim the moral authority accorded by the southern Pashtoon tribes to the clergy.

The issue of the Taliban's social and political standing is vital to understanding the movement's contemporary role. It is a movement that still largely retains control over the important social institutions of *masjid* (mosque) and madrassah. The spiritual authority asserted to its members means that they can win the cooperation and respect traditionally accorded to the mullahs. The movement has consistently projected a highly austere image, deliberately distancing itself from the extravagant and corrupt practices of previous rulers. But in its membership practices, the movement has been highly cliquish, granting admission to inner circles and according full respect to only those who share the *masjid*-madrassah origins of the leadership.

The Taliban cannot be considered to represent any of the tribes as each of the tribes from which the movement has recruited also has a hierarchy of elders and traditional leaders—a hierarchy often supplemented by a "new" leadership of commanders who emerged during the jihad and civil war and staked the first claim to becoming the post-1992 ruling elite. Part of the essence of the political practice of the Taliban movement has been its displacement of the mujahideen commander networks and its subjugation of the tribal networks in areas where the Taliban have asserted themselves. In their heyday, the Taliban famously swept aside the dominant commanders of the south and pushed the traditional tribal leadership into a subservient position. In constructing their relationship with the tribes in this way, the Taliban have departed from the familiar Pashtoon model of relationship building between tribal and clerical authority in periods of revolt.[2] But today, by virtue of the movement's base within the *masjids* and madrassahs, the Taliban retain a presence and influence throughout the Pashtoon areas, even where they are not militarily dominant.

As the insurgency has escalated, reports have frequently come from areas supposedly controlled by the government that describe how senior Taliban (and former Harakat-i-Inqilab or Haqani-linked) figures have traveled through the villages, conducting meetings in madrassahs and supporters' homes in their version of political outreach, mobilizing people for jihad. The same traditional tribal hierarchy that the government seeks to bind to its area administration simultaneously hosts Taliban envoys and pledges to cooperate in the Taliban's jihad.

Under current conditions, the Taliban have four potential claims to some political standing:

1. The Taliban themselves, consisting of those who have sworn loyalty to Mullah Omar and who remain active within the networks, constitute one of the largest organized movements in the country.
2. The Taliban, through Afghan and jihadi associates in the wider Deobandi madrassah network, have access to a large and renewable potential reserve of fresh supporters and activists.
3. Beyond their ability to deploy activists, the Taliban can penetrate and exert political and moral influence on the general population across much of southern Afghanistan. Through their base in the *masjids* and local madrassahs, they are able to place their supporters physically in any area they wish and are guaranteed both a welcome and a hearing.

2. David Edwards, *Before the Taliban: Genealogies of the Afghan Jihad* (Berkeley, CA: University of California Press, 2002).

4. Beyond influencing or intimidating the population, the Taliban have occasionally demonstrated the ability to outmaneuver the other elites and mobilize the population when they articulate a popular cause.

Although none of these factors constitutes liberal democratic credentials or tribal legitimacy, these factors do indicate that the Taliban may prove resilient and neutralize the influence of a weak administration in areas which they target. In modeling the Taliban and their influence, it is perhaps easier to describe what they are not. They are not simply a terrorist organization, a tribal movement, or a modern party. Rather, they are best considered a vanguardist brotherhood. They are in the vanguard in the sense that they assert moral authority over the general population, and they are a brotherhood in the sense that they have a strong awareness of identity and solidarity.

The Taliban and Terrorism: Ramifications for Reconciliation

To capture power in Afghanistan, the Taliban depended on a mixture of conventional military action and political intrigue. They also selectively employed terrorist tactics and famously harbored terrorists. The UN Security Council imposed sanctions on the Taliban movement for the latter sin, prompting the registry of Taliban-associated figures, which the United Nations still maintains. However, in the post-2001 insurgency, the Taliban have been even more dependent on tactics that by any definition constitute acts of terrorism, including targeted assassinations of civilian figures and bomb attacks on civilian targets or on military targets without due precautions to prevent civilian casualties. Furthermore, unlike armed movements elsewhere, the Taliban have failed to develop any parallel civilian entity that could distance itself from the violence but articulate the political concerns and demands of the movement. All institutions developed by the Taliban during the insurgency, including the regional *shuras*, the commissions, the district police chiefs and administrators who constitute their shadow government, the fronts, and the informal networks relate to the movement's armed activities. Even if some functions are specialized and compartmentalized, such as suicide-bomber training, no active part of the movement is really disassociated from the violence. Even inactive elements of the movement—for example, figures who have a background in the Taliban but who now have no operational association with the movement—prove remarkably reluctant to condemn their peers' terrorist tactics.

The Taliban's stubborn refusal to adjust to the changes of the post-2001 world poses enormous political and practical challenges for any reconciliation track. In consequence, there is no credible political proxy for the Taliban with which the government could pursue a dialogue to create the conditions for reconciliation. Direct engagement by the government with any part of the Taliban movement or insurgent networks risks being portrayed as having truck with terrorists, and the resultant political controversy could undermine any initiative. Ironically, however, the absence of a Taliban political wing seems to be an outcome of decisions by both the Afghanistan government and the Taliban.

From the Taliban side there was a failure of leadership. The "hardliners" were content to focus on the armed struggle. The moderates hoped for encouragement from the Afghan government, and in its absence were paralyzed. The first attempt by the Taliban to set up a peaceful political entity after 2001 was launched by Mawlvi Arsala Rahmani, who established Khadim ul Furqan, a revival of the prewar forerunner of the jihadi *tanzeem* Harakat-i-Inqilab. Operating from Islamabad, Arsala sought the blessing of the Afghan government to return to Afghanistan and use his party as a vehicle to bring the Taliban of the southeast peacefully into the new system. The government withheld this permission for almost three years and when it finally did invite Arsala and his associates to shift to Kabul, their activities were far too curbed to allow for any strategically significant impact. Arsala received a house in Kabul, a Senate seat, and chairmanship of a Senate committee and settled down to become just another former mujahid and Taliban who had reconciled with the government.

The other figure who entertained some aspirations to lead a Taliban political faction was former foreign minister Wakil Ahmad Mutawakil. After his release from detention in Bagram, the ever-optimistic Mutawakil expected that both the Taliban and the government would seize upon his presence in Kabul as an opportunity for bridge building. The

option of encouraging Mutawakil to develop an Afghan version of Pakistan's Jamiat Ulema Islami (Assembly of Islamic Clergy, or JUI) was
actively discussed within NSC circles. Indeed, although JUI factions
draw on a base of support in the same Deobandi madrassahs from which
the Afghan Taliban emerged, they are very much a part of the political
establishment in Pakistan. The NSC rationale was that it was inevitable
that such a party would eventually emerge in Afghanistan and that the
best hope for ensuring that it would become a constructive part of the
new political system was to preempt the process and install a reliable
leadership. However, this project was never pursued, no doubt because
its proponents realized that they would be vulnerable to accusations of
giving succor to the enemy. Indeed, despite its democratic credentials,
Pakistan's JUI (Fazal-ur-Rehman) party has routinely been described as
"the enemy" in Afghan intelligence briefings, a strong indication of the
trouble that the NSC would have found itself in if it had decided to back
Mutawakil. Although Mutawakil eventually did try to enter politics, his
decision to stand as an independent parliamentary candidate in the
highly tribalized environment of Kandahar was ill-conceived, undersup-
ported, and doomed to failure.

Insider-Outsider Dynamics

One of the greatest obstacles to reconciliation and a key political driver
of the conflict has been the country's insider-outsider dynamic. In short,
many of those who found themselves in power in the system that
emerged after 2001 benefited from maintaining the Taliban as a hostile
force and the main threat to the regime. Some of the crudest versions
of the insider-outsider dynamic occurred in the first year of the process
as local and national elites were still consolidating power. For example,
Defense Minister Marshall Faheem, while arguing for support for his
grossly inflated militias, talked up the threat of the Taliban reappearing
at the gates of Kabul. Local allies of Jamiat-i-Islami in the Pashtoon
areas won backing for security operations against their rivals by labeling
them as Taliban. The first major operation of Engineer Arif's NDS was
to round up hundreds of people associated with Hezb-i-Islami in Kabul
on the implausible pretext of a coup plot. (At the time it was clear from
contacts between Hezb-i-Islami figures and the United Nations that

they sought greater political inclusion, not a coup. This action only set back this process of inclusion.) In Kandahar, Urozgan, and Helmand, meanwhile, the new administration appointed former mujahideen figures whose previous disastrous rule had been brought to an end by the Taliban in 1994. They promptly began an interminable chase for "terrorists," driving out the Taliban who had thought that they could reintegrate peacefully and preside over the revival of the narcotics trade.

Although no one simple tribal formula describes who is in government and who is in opposition in the tribalized southwest, generally speaking, the stronger Durrani tribes quickly dominated the administration and security forces while the Ghilzai tribes and weaker Durrani tribes found themselves relatively marginalized. Despite the Taliban's background as a supratribal movement, Taliban figures frequently claimed after 2001 that the government side had launched a tribal conflict by unleashing the Durranis against the Ghilzais. Accordingly, the Taliban recruited from the outsiders, and a disproportionate share of their post-2001 forces in greater Kandahar came from the Ghilzais and the marginalized Durrani tribes.

After 2004, when electoral considerations started to have some impact on national politics, insider-outsider dynamics became more complex. The most obvious consequence of this was the successful initiative to co-opt a substantial Hezb-i-Islami faction into the system. Prior to 2004, Taliban and Hezb-i-Islami were vilified in almost equal measure. However, this started to change in the run-up to the presidential elections. By the time of the parliamentary elections, Hezb-i-Islami had effectively shed its outsider status. Because the party had sufficient numbers of its veterans placed in senior positions in the administration, its patronage links were as good as any of the other mujahideen factions.

There has been no such change in the Taliban's outsider status. With the rise of the insurgency, the trickle of middle- or senior-level Taliban figures being rehabilitated more or less dried up. The only former Taliban figure to benefit from executive patronage and receive senior appointment in the administration was Abdul Hakeem Munib, who was sent to Urozgan as governor. None was appointed to command positions in the new security forces, although a small cluster of former

Taliban was maintained in the Supreme Court. Despite the dilution of the factional control of the police and civil administration, the tribal and *masjid*-madrassah circles from which the Taliban have recruited remain outsiders to the system.

5

Recent Reconciliation Initiatives

Although the Afghan government has sporadically expressed support for reconciliation, this support has not been located within a coherent strategic framework. There has been a series of initiatives to promote reconciliation, but there has been no clear doctrine that lays out how the different components relate to one another or to other elements of strategy. In this sense, the country's post-2001 approach to reconciliation differs from the post-1986 PDPA approach, where pursuit of national reconciliation became a dominant theme of government action in multiple fields.

The range of loosely connected initiatives to promote reconciliation since 2001 has included both generic programs for all comers and tailored invitations to specific groups and individuals. To date, the principal officially endorsed initiatives include

- below-the-radar diplomacy by the NSC, including the Saudi process;
- high-profile diplomacy by the president;
- the PTS certification program;
- political outreach by the provincial governors;
- declaratory reconciliation by the Parliament through the "amnesty bill";
- atmospheric reconciliation through the Regional Peace Jirga;
- factional reconciliation through the Hezb-i-Islami track; and
- the establishment of reconciliation principles by the Policy Action Group (PAG).[1]

Below-the-Radar Diplomacy by the NSC

The NSC was established to provide strategic guidance for a range of government security organs. In terms of policymaking and

---

1. For a comparative analysis of reconciliation initiatives that have generated a certain amount of operating experience, see appendix B.

coordination, it is the body that brings together those responsible for leading the police, army, intelligence service, and civil administration. In addition to its strategic work, the NSC has been able to undertake security tasks prioritized by the president. Soon after its inception, the NSC began utilizing this operational capacity to conduct discreet diplomacy with insurgent networks. Although the principal objective is to persuade significant insurgent figures to engage in open reconciliation, the NSC's work of probing the insurgent networks has helped to maintain a channel of communication between the presidential team and the insurgent leadership. This channel has not resulted in immediate changes of stance, but it may be of potential benefit to future reconciliation.

The NSC's close working relationship with the president is especially important because all top-level reconciliation to date has had "executive sponsorship." Indeed, the NSC channel has been used to facilitate the reconciliation of the handful of senior Taliban figures, including Rais Abdul Wahid of Baghran, Helmand; Mawlvi Arsala Rahmani of Paktika; Mullah Mujahid and Rahmatullah Sangaryar of Urozgan; and former Radio Shariat director Mullah Ishaq Nizami. The reconciliation of figures of this level of seniority requires important security decisions to be taken before their arrival, and their aftercare requires government actions, both to support them and to "exploit" them. For example, Nizami, as a former Taliban propagandist, was an obvious source of insight into how public information might be made more relevant to an audience of potential reconcilers.

Locating this high-value reconciliation work within the NSC makes sense because of its coordination and liaison responsibilities with the other security bodies. However, the NSC has never operated its reconciliation facility at a scale likely to achieve strategic impact. Indeed, its caseload has been extremely limited. The government has established this facility and demonstrated that it is the most effective available tool to promote serious reconciliation only to then fail to give it the proper resources or to make full use of it. This suggests that, despite the rhetoric, making tangible progress on reconciliation is a low-order policy priority. The NSC team has been at pains to stress that the preferred reconciliation channel is the PTS. However, from the time of the launch of the PTS, the NSC has had no illusions about the poor prospects for achieving any significant reconciliation through the PTS. The NSC has successfully processed those figures it has been tasked to reconcile, but it does not seem to have been under pressure to up the numbers or to make a greater strategic impact.

High-Profile Presidential Diplomacy

The most visible face of reconciliation for much of the country has been the public diplomacy conducted by President Karzai himself. This diplomacy consists of periodic restatements of commitment to the idea of reconciliation and the president personally welcoming back insurgent figures whom he has specifically targeted for reconciliation. The most well-known of the presidential initiatives has included Karzai's January 2006 plea to Mullah Omar and Gulbadin Hekmatyar to leave the insurgency and to return to Afghanistan to live in peace. In a slightly different vein, the president publicly welcomed reconciled insurgent Mullah Abdul Salaam, a former Taliban provincial governor. Salaam declared his loyalty to the government in advance of the operation to recapture Musa Qala in December 2007, and the president reciprocated by appointing him as district administrator.

Although the president seems to be interested in projecting a general readiness to reconcile in his public diplomacy, his public appeals are not intended to contribute to securing deals with the figures to whom they are addressed. Indeed, such public diplomacy has no connection with the government's more discreet reconciliation channels. In this sense, the public appeals to Mullah Omar represent theatrical gestures (perhaps in the tradition of similar gestures made by Amin and Karmal). They are made with no expectation that they will positively influence Mullah Omar or others to whom they are addressed, because there is no evidence of insurgents being swayed by such public appeals. In fact, because their rebuttals to date have consistently denounced the "puppet regime" in Kabul, any figure who makes a public appeal for reconciliation knows what response to expect. Furthermore, the credibility of the public appeals has been undermined by instances of rapid retractions. For example, Karzai's very first such appeal and announcement of an amnesty for Taliban made on December 6, 2001, was immediately contradicted by the coalition. Overall, the government's public diplomacy on reconciliation lacks substance and strategic coherence.

The PTS Certification Program

The principal vehicle used for officially endorsed reconciliation is the Independent National Commission for Peace, headed by Professor Sebghatullah Mojadedi. This commission was launched in May 2005 by presidential decree and has been given the responsibility of administering the PTS. The commission and its flagship projects are examples of reconciliation initiatives that scrupulously avoid adopting the Communist-era *ashti milli* terminology, despite the similarities to the program launched under Najib in 1986. The main role of the commission has been to certify that former insurgents are living peacefully and have accepted the new constitution. It carries out this role by running a network of field offices in insurgency-affected provinces. Staff members in the field offices and in Kabul are charged with identifying and persuading combatants to come under the umbrella of the PTS. The reconciled combatants then meet with Professor Mojadedi and receive a letter from him stating that they have reconciled, which they are tasked with taking to their provincial governor for countersignature.

The commission generates a significant amount of media coverage that publicizes the reconciliation events. In some cases, combatants joining the program have been shown on television handing in their weapons. In addition to its "general" program of reconciliation, the commission has been responsible for administering a reentry program for suspected insurgents released from U.S. detention in Guantanamo or Bagram. Batches of returnees have been feted by the commission and issued their certificates. Alongside the certification program, the commission runs a guest house in Kabul that allows it to accommodate people joining the program who are arriving from Pakistan or the provinces. This is very much in the tradition of the Communist-era national reconciliation program's iconic "peace guest house." The commission has several times proposed to launch economic rehabilitation activities for reconciled insurgents. However, it has been unable to secure the resources to launch such activities on a meaningful scale. The commission also operates as a security liaison, coordinating with the NDS on potential security issues raised by those who join the program

Alongside the presidential appeals, the commission has become the other public face of reconciliation, starting with Mojadedi's enthusiastic but controversial announcement of an amnesty for Mullah Omar and Gulbadin Hekmatyar in his inaugural speech. Indeed, judged by crude throughput, the PTS is the only program that has operated on a scale that promises strategic impact. The commission has also been the main repository of international investment in reconciliation. Up to the end of 2007, the commission had certified some five thousand people as having reconciled. However, there is a significant gap between reality and the claimed effectiveness of the commission's work.

The first and fundamental issue relates to the credibility of the combatant- or insurgent-related status professed by those who have taken up the reconciliation offer. The absence of a formal evaluation of the PTS throughput hinders assessment of their actual status. Consistent anecdotal evidence indicates that the great majority of those passing through the PTS system have not recently been involved in conflict, which for all intents and purposes makes their laying down of arms meaningless. A perusal of the PTS records indicates that almost no previously known insurgents have participated in the program. (The author personally reviewed the reports of all 4,634 individuals who had entered the program by October 2007.) Although a handful of known insurgents have "graduated" from the program, they were either referred by another organ (the NSC channel) or introduced to the program upon release from custody. Given that the security guarantee implied by the PTS certificate can only be of use for those who were previously associated with the insurgency, it is not exactly clear why noninsurgents are associating themselves with the program. There is a small financial incentive for participation in the program through the provision of a tiny travel grant, but in many cases, it seems that individuals may be signing up simply to do a favor to the PTS staff to help them fill up their numbers and thus justify their claims on the central budget.

Apart from the lack of relevant recruits to the PTS, the program has suffered from numerous other drawbacks, including a credibility gap. Although the PTS certificate is not meant to offer immunity in the event of future misdemeanors, it is supposed to accord a kind of "person-of-special-interest" status to the bearer. The letter includes contact phone numbers so that relatives of the reconciled insurgent—or even security forces—know how to contact the program in the event that the individual finds himself in trouble. In reality, however, security forces and law enforcement officials have shown little interest in the PTS letters. As a result, anyone certified as reconciled is just as vulnerable to arbitrary arrest or harassment as anyone who has not been through the program.

Additionally, the PTS has been unable to offer serious post-reconciliation services, an issue which would become even more significant if the PTS ever had to deal with a caseload of people who really had been involved with the insurgency. For example, one of the practical problems in achieving the reintegration of real insurgents is that they are frequently the subject of false reports to security agencies that state that they still represent a security threat. In such cases where PTS clients have faced harassment, the commission has found it difficult to mount effective backup for them.

The commission has struggled even to maintain the quality of its basic reception services. Over the years, there have been persistent complaints of poor living conditions and inadequate, low-quality food at the program's guest house. Although this may seem a minor matter, numerous Taliban-associated figures have commented on how a shoddy reception undermines the confidence that is fundamental to any real reconciliation. A rare mid-level Taliban figure came to the guest house but left the program in protest, unhappy with the poor reception services.

The commission claims to have extensive relations with senior figures in the insurgency and periodically gives alerts that it is on the brink of reconciling them. For example, the commission claims to have been on the brink of reconciling Dadaullah at the time of his demise. Likewise, the commission claims that its five thousand clients predominantly represent fighters whom it successfully wooed away from the conflict, but there is no empirical basis for such tall claims.

Despite these problems, the commission seems to serve three functions. First, it is symbolic of an official commitment to reconciliation, similar to the president's public gestures. It is the one organ consistently repeating that there is an official policy of encouraging insurgents to leave the armed struggle and reintegrate. Second, it offers a vehicle for accommodating within the system and dispensing patronage to one progovernment network—that is, those directly associated with the leadership of the commission. Third, it provides a public forum for welcoming back significant figures who have been reconciled through more direct channels, such as through the NSC. Beyond these three functions, however, there is no evidence that the commission has either the inclination or capacity to establish links with strategically significant parts of the insurgency or to reach a reconciliatory understanding with them.

In light of all this, it is illuminating to recall the three specific program risks that this author identified at the time that the PTS was launched: (1) only politically and militarily insignificant people might avail of the invitation because the Taliban still favored armed resistance and would thus effectively block the scheme; (2) the Taliban who did choose to reconcile might face difficulties in integration because of the ineffectiveness or hostility of the local administration in the areas to which they returned; (3) critics of the government might politicize the process by misportraying the reintegration process as a threat to the balance of power or to democracy.[2]

Of these three identified risks, the first has clearly materialized, as evidenced by this author's study of the case reports and by the significant escalation of the insurgency and the increase in the number of active antigovernment militants. There is relatively little anecdotal evidence to suggest that the second risk has materialized, possibly because of the lack of real militants in the caseload. Even so, several reconciled individuals have complained of a lack of support and a general apathy—that is, they feel marginalized and acutely aware that they do not belong to any strong patronage network within the state, which is popularly considered as a key to prosperity and security in Afghanistan. The third risk has not yet become a major issue because of the paucity of high-profile and strategically sensitive individuals availing of PTS.

Political Outreach by the Provincial Governors

The provincial governors play a key strategic role in the Afghan administrative system as they coordinate all civilian departments and security organs within the provinces. In particular, they chair the provincial

---

2. These risks were laid out by the author in a memo prepared for the European Union special representative at the time of the PTS launch in 2005.

security committees and have outreach to all provincial districts through their management of the district administrators (*uluswal*s). They also deal with the public, receive delegations, and attend *jirga*s.

In 2007 the government recognized the contribution that all governors make to stabilization through the process of political outreach by mobilizing funds to support them in this work. By actively engaging with key stakeholders, such as tribal elders, commanders, and religious figures throughout their provinces, the governors are able to approach and co-opt potential opposition figures. The national budget now includes a financial provision for the governors' outreach activities, providing them with funds to facilitate the work of *jirga*s and envoys. Prior to the initiation of this transparent process, governors in insurgency-affected provinces or with political clout received even larger allocations of "operational funds" for security-related activities, which at times included wooing opposition figures.

Although there has been no systematic documentation of the effectiveness of the governors' work on reconciliation, their work clearly has the potential to have a strategic impact. There are promising examples of governors in insurgency-affected provinces proactively launching local initiatives either to achieve reconciliation with significant insurgent networks or to mobilize passive or estranged tribes to exclude insurgent networks from their areas. For example, the Musa Qala Accord in 2006, which gave control of a district center to the local tribal *jirga*, officially started as a governor's initiative and was signed by the governor of Helmand and the district's tribal elders. Asadullah Khalid, while serving as governor of Kandahar, tasked agents to penetrate insurgent networks and directly approached some of the Taliban commanders to cooperate with him. The governor of Zabul has both conducted his own diplomacy with insurgent networks and approached border tribes, seeking their cooperation in excluding insurgents. The governor of Paktia established *jirga*s in areas subject to infiltration from Waziristan and has dispatched envoys to top insurgent leader Siraj Haqani. And the governor of Kunar held a series of local border *jirga*s, winning promises of cooperation from tribes and administration on the Pakistani side of the border, while the governor of Urozgan has called his own version of a peace *jirga*.[3]

---

3. These examples were encountered by the author while undertaking political reporting

The anecdotal evidence of governor activity indicates that the provincial administrations of all the main insurgency-affected provinces have been launching reconciliation-oriented activities that address strategic priorities, such as engaging top insurgent leaders and addressing infiltration from the main centers of the insurgency. The reality is that such efforts have not resulted in overt reconciliation and that the escalation of the insurgency that began in 2005 occurred despite the efforts of governors toward provincial-level reconciliation. Basic security indicators on increasing levels of insurgency activity indicate that none of the governors has been able to reverse the escalatory trend, which suggests that the governors alone do not hold any miraculous solution for reconciliation to win the war. On the other hand, the governor-initiated reconciliation initiatives have been uncoordinated, unsupported, unrecognized, and basically separate from what was supposed to be the national program on reconciliation, the PTS. In this sense, it can be argued that the full potential of the subnational administration to contribute to reconciliation has never been tested.

Declaratory Reconciliation by the Parliament

The Parliament launched its own reconciliation initiative in the form of a resolution adopted on January 31, 2007, titled "The Charter for Compromise and National Reconciliation." Adopted in the wake of controversy stirred up by the president's endorsement of a strategy for "transitional justice,"[4] this "amnesty bill" is a medley of loosely connected points that includes even a direct denunciation of Human Rights Watch, whose press release on the occasion of the launch of the transitional justice strategy became the focus of controversy. The parliamentary resolution was correctly portrayed as a move by war crimes suspects in the Parliament to provide themselves with immunity in the event that transitional justice entailed prosecutions. Despite the dubious antecedents of the charter, however, it provides an interesting statement of reconciliation as shaped by the former combatants in Parliament.

---

in the insurgency-affected provinces.

4. Afghanistan Independent Human Rights Commission, *Peace, Reconciliation and Justice in Afghanistan: Action Plan of the Government of the Islamic Republic of Afghanistan* (Kabul: AIHRC, 2005).

For precedent, the charter cites both the Prophet Mohammad's sparing of his defeated enemies as he victoriously entered Mecca, as well as the reconciliation that occurred in South Africa and Tajikistan. It announced an amnesty to members of all factions from all different stages of the conflict and called on members of the armed opposition to embrace reconciliation. In concept the initiative was inclusive, transparent, based on an approach of co-option, and specifically involved no international involvement. It was notable for the way in which regime "insiders," the old Northern Alliance commanders in Parliament, publicly associated themselves with a call for the Taliban to reconcile. However, it offered a disturbing prospect of a return to the false dichotomy of peace versus justice, and it was predictably fated to remain a controversial declaration rather than a law that could be implemented. In reality, the reconciliation committee has never been activated, so passage of the bill has not led to any practical measures or tangible reconciliation.

Atmospheric Reconciliation through the Regional Peace Jirga

In July 2007 Kabul hosted a joint *jirga* with a large delegation from Pakistan's Pashtoon areas. The declared objectives of the *jirga* were to promote friendly relations between the two countries and work for reconciliation of those engaged in conflict. The run-up to the holding of the *jirga* was anything but conciliatory, with protracted tactical play between the leaderships of both countries over whether and when the *jirga* would be held. Despite the initial tactical play, the *jirga* was formally successful. Both countries assigned credible delegations, including a cross section of their political classes and a range of government and civil-society figures. Resolutions called for a lasting improvement in relations and delegates agreed to a follow-up mechanism that would include tasking representatives to pursue practical reconciliation by engaging with figures close to the insurgency.

However, the contribution of the *jirga* has been limited to the positive atmospherics that arose at the time that it was held. The promised follow-up has been limited and delayed. In August 2008, a planned "mini *jirga*," consisting of two national delegations that was a hybrid government–civil-society initiative, was convened in Islamabad. It resolved to initiate contacts with "opposition groups" in both countries in support of a process of dialogue for peace and contributed to legitimizing the idea of reconciliation, but there is no sign of executive commitment to implement anything resolved by the forum or to move it beyond atmospherics. In the absence of sustained backing by Kabul or Islamabad, the civil-society component has proven unable to take the initiative forward. As a result, the regional *jirga* remains another example of a reconciliation gesture that—although rather more elaborate and expensive than some previous ones—has failed to offer a realistic follow-up arrangement or to link to a practical process that could facilitate actual reconciliation.

Factional Reconciliation through the Hezb-i-Islami Track

The political engagement pursued by the government with Hezb-i-Islami since the end of 2001 offers a case study of what reconciliation might have been like had the Taliban opted to develop a political organization parallel to its insurgency. Much of the Afghan internal diplomacy during the 1990s focused on the search for a formula that would bind all major mujahideen factions, in particular Hezb-i-Islami and Jamiat-i-Islami, to a political settlement. The failure of this search led both to the civil war and to the rise of the Taliban. In 2001, there was a question over whether Hezb-i-Islami would support or oppose the new setup. On the one hand, many former Hezb-i-Islami figures participated in the final moves to topple the Taliban and clearly considered themselves to be part of the mujahideen elite who would step into the administration and security organs once the Taliban had been pushed aside. On the other hand, the faction's traditional rivals had the upper hand at Bonn and party leader Hekmatyar stood back from endorsing the internationally backed settlement. As early as December 2001, the president hosted the first Hezb-i-Islami delegation in Kabul to discuss its leadership's endorsement of the new setup. Even so, Hezb-i-Islami adopted a stance of strategic ambiguity in 2002 and 2003. Although Hekmatyar and a handful of former commanders went underground in Pakistan and associated themselves with the insurgency, the majority of former Hezb-i-Islami figures did indeed integrate relatively normally into the new setup and many of them were incorporated into the new government structures.

The first moves toward political reconciliation came in 2003 and 2004, in the early stages of the run-up to the presidential election. A caucus within the old Hezb-i-Islami leadership, many of them hitherto based in Peshawar, launched a process of talks with both the government and some of the government's international partners. They sought the legal status to be able to conduct peaceful political activities within Afghanistan and a guarantee of nonharassment and financial support so that they could establish themselves as a legitimate political party. The presidential team pursued this track, seeking a clear statement from the Hezb-i-Islami delegation that if they established themselves in Kabul they would clearly disassociate themselves from Gulbadin Hekmatyar, who was still "underground" and conducting proinsurgency propaganda.

As an outcome of the engagement, the faction was established in Kabul. The government discreetly provided it with financial backing and security, enabling it to establish an operating base in the city. The faction was also eventually registered with the Justice Ministry after a long wrangle over its name. There was some government resistance to the idea of registering a party by the name of Hezb-i-Islami, because this might imply recognition or endorsement of Hekmatyar. In support of this argument, government figures argued spuriously that Hezb-i-Islami was listed internationally as a terrorist organization. But if the purpose of the exercise was to co-opt former Hezb-i-Islami members into the new political system, it was important that the registered Hezb-i-Islami not only be lawful and peaceful but also look as much as possible like the "original" Hezb-i-Islami. A clue could have been taken from Hekmatyar's own position: he feared that registration of the faction as Hezb-i-Islami would weaken his own control.

In terms of providing a vehicle to facilitate the co-option of Hezb-i-Islami loyalists into the new setup, the move to register the faction has been relatively successful. It participated in the parliamentary elections and obtained a significant but not dominating presence in Parliament and has remained constructively involved in national politics. Furthermore, the peaceful presence of Hezb-i-Islami has significantly broadened the base of the political system. The faction has been successful in attracting most of the original Hezb-i-Islami leadership and has assisted in the process of ending harassment of former Hezbis, which was a major problem in 2002 and 2003 and risked promoting their recruitment into the insurgency in the same way that the predatory behavior of the southwestern administration drove Taliban into the insurgency.

Despite the warnings at the time of the launch of the dialogue that the registered faction would act as a Trojan horse for Hekmatyar in seeking to overthrow the government, there has been no evidence of any such possibility. Indeed, the peaceful operation of the faction in Kabul has served to marginalize both the militant faction within Hezb-i-Islami and Hekmatyar himself. The handling of Hezb-i-Islami arguably constitutes the most successful example of a reconciliation strategy so far pursued since Bonn. The process was successful in part because Hezb-i-Islami leaders themselves made the overtures, because the president saw political advantage in achieving an alliance with this faction, and because, in terms of their network links established over thirty years, the Hezb-i-Islami leaders were part of the informal mujahideen establishment. Although the network linkages of the Taliban are different and the significance of the remaining estranged Hezb-i-Islami leadership is disputed, the experience offers a relevant model of how a large network can be incorporated into the political process.

The Establishment of Reconciliation Principles

In April 2008 the executive tasked the national security adviser with developing a set of "reconciliation principles" to act as parameters to guide future initiatives. The United Nations Assistance Mission in Afghanistan (UNAMA) and the Policy Action Group, the main government-international joint security forum, produced several versions of these principles. A set of them was eventually agreed to that can be viewed as the Afghan government's official doctrine on reconciliation. As eloquently elaborated on by Mohammad Masoom Stanekzai, these principles fall into one of four broad sections.[5] The section that outlines "fundamental principles" states that all reconciliation efforts will be led

---

5. See Mohammad Masoom Stanekzai, *Thwarting Afghanistan's Insurgency: A Pragmatic Approach toward Peace and Reconciliation*, Special Report 212 (Washington, D.C.: United States Institute of Peace Press, September 2008).

by the Afghan government, with international support provided only as requested. It further states that reconcilees are to renounce violence and that no amnesty is to be granted. The section that outlines "process-related principles" states that prospective clients are to benefit from confidentiality, are to be subject to probationary monitoring, and are only eligible to a stake in government ("share in power") in accordance with the democratic process. The section that outlines "organizational and institutional principles" states that a reformed PTS is to be retained as the premier operational organ for reconciliation but that it will be supplemented by a "senior focal point" with a strong coordination function. The section that outlines "outreach-related principles" states that the government is to conduct public information to mobilize support for the reconciliation idea, establish contacts with insurgency-related groups, and develop support networks for reconcilees.

Several concerns initially drove the work to elaborate a set of reconciliation principles. There was a growing sense that, whereas international and national actors agreed on the need for reconciliation to be pursued, there was no common vision of what a successful reconciliation process would look like. The fragmented vision generated a risk of either paralysis or uncoordinated and self-defeating actions. A transparent set of principles is meant to make clear what everyone has signed up for and what the boundaries of legitimate action are. Furthermore, government or international support of reconciliation has at times been subject to harsh public criticism, often based on serious distortions of what was actually envisaged. The principles explicitly rule out unconstitutional power-sharing deals or amnesties in an attempt to deflect criticism that reconciliation amounts to capitulation. The government has also been concerned about the prospect of it losing control over reconciliation if local or international actors pursue uncoordinated initiatives. Additionally, international actors have been doubtful about the seriousness of government intent given its difficulty in spelling out precisely what it intended to do and what it wanted supported to further reconciliation.

The principles are significant because they represent the clearest statement yet of the state of thinking about reconciliation by the Afghan government and its international supporters. The most obvious contribution that the principles offer is a degree of reassurance to those who were concerned that reconciliation might subvert the established order in Afghanistan. The principles describe a minimalist approach to reconciliation, envisaging *co-option* of insurgents to the political system, with no threat of compromising the interests of insiders in this system. However, in appraising the likely contribution of the principles to achieving real progress on reconciliation, it is important to consider whether they address those constraints that have made progress to date so limited.

The principles are largely a restatement of security doctrine that has already been guiding government-led reconciliation since at least 2005. The NSC leadership already spelled out most of these principles when briefing partners on the launch of the PTS program in 2005. The NSC envisaged that the PTS would serve as the strong "focal point" that is now called for and that a steering group would guide the work of the PTS. However, as the analysis of PTS performance in this monograph indicates, the program has had a disturbing lack of strategic relevance. By retaining the PTS as the main operational organ for effecting reconciliation, the principles risk replicating failure. Although the principles state that the PTS will be "reformed," it is entirely unproven that the institution is amenable to reform.

The principles also include a strong restatement of the government-led approach, affirming that the government will have a monopoly on reconciliation-oriented contacts with the armed opposition. UNAMA has volunteered its good offices to assist the government-led reconciliation program, a move which would entail UNAMA providing the main international civilian political input for reconciliation. However, the principles clarify that any such role will be entirely subordinate: "the Afghan government may ask the United Nations and other international actors to provide support to Afghan-led reconciliation programs."[6] The assertion of a strong government lead in part reflects the general stance of Kabul since the Bonn transitional stage: it wants to be more clearly in charge of all programs. It also reflects the prevalent Afghan concern that international partners might be negotiating separate peaces that run counter to the government's view of the national interest.

---

6. Ibid., 13.

Ironically, the concern in 2005 was slightly different. Precisely because reconciliation was controversial, the government wanted to "spread the blame" by associating other actors with the process. The desire to broaden the ownership of reconciliation was one reason that the implementing organ was given independent status and put under the leadership of Sebghatullah Mojadedi, a respected jihadi leader, rather than kept as a government body. In the face of the reality of conflict in 2008, other considerations also began to have a bearing on the dynamics of the Afghan and international roles in reconciliation. As conflict has escalated, the administration's span of control and authority in insurgency-affected areas has contracted. As a result, the government has repeatedly been obliged to appoint divisive "strong man"-type figures in charge of district-level administration and security. In such circumstances, the credibility of a strictly government-led reconciliation approach is increasingly in doubt. An alternative would be to include a greater use of independent figures who enjoy both government confidence and greater coordination and transparency.

Overall, the reconciliation principles represent a restatement of ideas that might have contributed positively in 2005 if they had been applied seriously then. Given that they represent a repeat of an approach that has failed to deliver for three years, there would seem to be a case for a more radical overhaul of them. If the principles are to be adopted to cope with the latest challenges, they should incorporate a response to the constraints experienced in the first three years of formal reconciliation and to new opportunities. A well-coordinated failure is little more palatable than a poorly coordinated failure. Overhauled principles should include a broadening of the approach to include *accommodation* as well as *co-option*, abandoning failed implementation mechanisms, and incorporating some positive tactical lessons from experience to date.

6

Reflections on Reconciliation

Even if no single program has delivered a major breakthrough in reconciliation, there is now sufficient experience from the range of national and international efforts to derive some guidelines on what works and what does not work in establishing the conditions for success in reconciliation. The reflections presented here draw on the author's personal experience of conducting reconciliation-oriented political contacts and assessing other reconciliation initiatives.

Individual versus Group Approaches

One of the reasons for the limited acceptance of official offers of reconciliation is that the government's reconciliation program, as operationalized, has been oriented to individual insurgents. An individualized approach flies in the face of the way that the insurgency is organized, which involves a critical role for comrade-solidarity networks. Participation in the insurgency does not imply individual membership to a modern political organization, which the individual is free to leave at any time without constraint. Rather, participation in the insurgency is an outcome of an individual's belonging to a network with which he shares beliefs, values, fraternal bonds, and, through patronage links, economic interests. Any reconciliation process that builds upon an understanding of the way the insurgency works would seek to bring over not the individual but the network.

A group approach to reconciliation has a greater likelihood of success, because any individual insurgent would be more willing to reconcile if he could still enjoy the solidarity gained from belonging to his comrade network after reconciliation. Additionally, it has the potential to have a greater impact than an individual approach, because it removes the building blocks of the insurgency, which would be difficult for recalcitrant insurgents to replace. Aside from the sociological reasons in favor of group reconciliation, there are very practical reasons for believing that a group approach stands the most chance of success. In keeping with the Taliban tradition of ruthlessness, any insurgent living in an area where other insurgents are active would come under immediate threat of being targeted by them should he decide to reconcile. Network-based reconciliation, in which all those affiliated with a network reconcile simultaneously, and area-based reconciliation, in which a cluster of insurgents from a contiguous area reconcile simultaneously, offer the prospect of collective security. Former insurgents extricating themselves from the conflict with the government can be empowered to make security arrangements for themselves, their networks, and their areas to protect against any recalcitrant insurgents. This model is close to the protocol pursued by the Afghan government before 1992. It acknowledges that in an ongoing conflict there is no single step to take combatants out of the fight.

A group approach to reconciliation requires a more complex architecture and expects those personnel charged with pursuing reconciliation to engage with the group and to make detailed arrangements to facilitate the successful reintegration of the group. Such arrangements can include establishing lines of communication with local administration and security forces, recruiting personnel into security forces, arranging employment, and obtaining arms licenses. This is a more politically demanding process than dispensing a standard individual package. Although some of the provincial governors and regional offices of the PTS program have come close to a group or area approach in which they have worked to bring distinct armed groups into the program, there has been no systematic support for or encouragement of group reconciliation. The reality is that neither the Afghan government nor the political presence of the international community has had the capacity or inclination to pursue this kind of engagement with an insurgent network, which is one reason why many insurgents amenable to exiting the conflict have continued to fight.

The Joined-up Approach

Insurgents who have expressed an interest in reconciliation have cited numerous reasons for entering the armed struggle, including grievances against the government and pressure from the strongmen who control administration and security at the local level. They also have cited the need to find a livelihood, a desire for some form of security, mistrust of the government security forces, and a basic identification with the political and religious arguments for jihad advanced by insurgent propagandists as reasons for joining the insurgency. To enable networks to extricate themselves from the insurgency, it is important to address the range of factors that motivate participation in it. It is wholly inadequate to address only one factor, such as individual security, as PTS generally does. Indeed, providing credible political and security guarantees against harassment, mobilizing a meaningful livelihood package, inducting former combatants into a local security arrangement, troubleshooting when problems occur, and monitoring all activities requires a wide spectrum of actions that are beyond the scope of any single national or international government agency. The PTS program was never empowered to the extent to be able to undertake collective action. No official program charged with reconciliation has ever been given a mandate to undertake collective action across security, economic, and political sectors. That said, the Afghan government has shown its ability to conduct such collective action when the task is deemed a high-enough priority. However, this has happened only on an ad hoc basis. The support provided by the government to Mullah Abdul Salaam in December 2007 is a prime example of this. Because of a presidential endorsement, a reconciled insurgent and his supporters were provided with security, logistical support, and economic assistance; they even received a case officer to manage them. The failure to institutionalize this collective approach has severely handicapped all other attempts at reconciliation.

Political Patronage

Reconciliation successes, in which senior military or political figures associated with the armed opposition have reconciled and come under the authority of the Afghan government, have generally involved the participation of a senior political patron. Both the Mullah Abdul Salaam and Abdul Wahid Baghrani cases demonstrate that clear presidential backing or patronage can be a powerful incentive in persuading insurgent figures to accept reconciliation. Those senior Taliban figures who reconciled in the early post-2001 period did so on the basis of assurances issued to them by figures inside the new government with whom they had a relationship of trust. Their contacts informally acted as patrons or guarantors.

There are numerous counterexamples in which insurgents seeking reconciliation gave up and returned to the safety of their networks because they concluded that no one on the government side was committed to winning them over or would be willing to defend their interests after they reconciled. Another reason that potential reconcilers have forgone the process has been the lack of any patron within the government who belongs to their networks and in whom they could trust. As a result, many of them have felt alienated from government structures.

Strategic Approaches

The cluttering of the reconciliation process with individuals who have no recent history of involvement in conflict, who are of no relevance to peacemaking, and who have no need to reconcile with anyone is a problem that has assumed strategic dimensions. The low percentage of serious clients in the PTS program renders any further investment in such a program virtually meaningless. The basic lesson drawn from the PTS experience is that any program offering even the most minor incentives for reconciliation risks being swamped by candidates of zero strategic significance. The prevalence of tactical behavior (whereby individuals associated with the insurgency only pretend to be interested in reconciliation for their own benefit) and disinformation (whereby individuals impersonate a category of actor deemed to be a priority in order to receive assistance) is such that unless there is a strict strategic orientation to a reconciliation program resources will be needlessly diverted and the credibility of the program will be undermined. The most effective remedy to this problem is to ensure that the reconciliation work is analysis driven. Contacts must be proactively established with prioritized insurgent networks, and approaches to or from reconciliation candidates should only be entertained after their standing and strategic significance are established. To ensure that a program retains strategic focus, its output and allocation of resources must be independently assessed. Post-2001 reconciliation initiatives have been singularly lacking in strategic direction.

Military Pressure

The debate over whether reconciliation equals appeasement raises interesting questions about the relationship between military force and reconciliation. For example, Tehreek-i-Taliban Pakistan militants have consistently linked their own willingness to enter negotiations with their demands for cease-fires and the withdrawal of the Pakistan Army from areas where the army has launched operations. As a result, government peace initiatives, such as the 2008 and 2009 Swat agreements, have been portrayed as compromising the military effort. Critics have argued that agreement on any terms other than capitulation amounts to appeasement and so military action must always be continued to the point where the government can negotiate from a position of strength—and thus secure capitulation.

In-conflict reconciliation entails a rather more sophisticated relationship between military effort and political engagement with the insurgents. It was clear from some of the author's insurgent dialogues that stepped-up military pressure by the International Security Assistance Force (ISAF) through the targeting of mid- and high-level commanders did make many commanders willing to talk. They wanted to find a way out. But it was equally clear that, even in the face of immediate military threat, they retained a range of concerns, including a desire to preserve honor and self-respect. If capitulation was the only option, they were prepared to take their chances on the battlefield.

A credible military threat may indeed concentrate the minds of insurgents trying to find a way out of the conflict. But the desired peaceful outcome depends on the credibility of the reconciliation process and the terms on offer. For reconciliation to be credible to both sides, it is important that it offer the reconciling insurgents and their area or network real protection from the military threat and that the reconciled commanders' obligations to maintain area security are clearly established and subject to monitoring.

Until such time as a general peace agreement becomes attainable, military force and political engagement do not equate to victory and appeasement, respectively. Rather, both military force and a reconciliation process should be pursued smartly and complementarily.

Reconciled Commanders and Photo Opportunities

There are both international and national dimensions to the current insurgency—one conflict among Afghans over the composition of the new ruling elite and another conflict between some Afghans and international forces over the nature of the international intervention in the country. As a result, issues related to how reconciliation is presented affect whether it will be palatable for all reconciling parties and whether it will prove sustainable. Additionally, there is a tension between the visibility of a reconciliation process and the likelihood of it achieving strategic effect, especially in the early stages when confidence in the process must still be established. Any figure directly or indirectly associated with the insurgency faces the possibility of retribution for establishing unauthorized contacts with either government or international allies. Therefore, any serious interlocutor should be averse to publicity and should maintain discretion even over contacts. This concern applies all the more to contacts with internationals.

Active insurgents contemplating reconciliation have a range of preferences regarding how long they would want their contacts to be kept confidential. In the Mullah Abdul Salaam case, once he received presidential backing and was lobbying for material assistance, he was prepared to interact openly with both the government and the ISAF and to be the subject of publicity. However, most insurgents would prefer to maintain a low profile for a longer period and would prefer to maintain a visible distance from any internationals. That said, the political context within which they are reconciling can affect their preferences. Insurgents who are concerned about tribal grievances, for example, tend to welcome some visible ISAF association when reconciling, because they want additional protection against harassment. Insurgents who have been mobilized to fight against the foreign troop presence, meanwhile, tend to make their reconciliation with the Afghan government virtually conditional upon being allowed to maintain a visible distance from international forces. In the end, whether there are photo opportunities for reconciled commanders to pose beside ISAF commanders has no bearing on the strategic value of a network that has agreed to end hostilities.

7

International Support for Reconciliation

T he logic of the Bonn Accords, with its affirmation of Afghan sovereignty and placement of international actors in a supporting role to the Afghan government, applies to reconciliation initiatives, too. Although the international community has been generally supportive of the idea of reconciliation in Afghanistan, it has been chronically unable to support it in ways that would achieve strategic impact. Because the PTS was launched as the government's flagship reconciliation initiative, it has been the most obvious recipient for such support and, accordingly, has received funds and technical assistance from the international community. Aside from this support to the PTS, however, the international community has made efforts to support reconciliation on a handful of other fronts.

UNAMA and the PRTs

In 2007, UNAMA tentatively developed a concept of political outreach as its direct contribution to reconciliation. UNAMA political officers had already been tasked with maintaining contacts at all levels of society, including with those indirectly associated with the insurgency. Several commanders in insurgency-affected areas had approached UNAMA expressing a desire to extricate themselves from the conflict, but they had a lack of confidence in the ability of available government counterparts to manage the negotiation process toward peaceful rehabilitation. The thought was that UNAMA could use its good offices in support of government objectives to engage with such figures as a first step before linking them up with the administration and official reconciliation apparatus. In this way, UNAMA could act as a peaceful "force multiplier" for the government and capitalize on its reasonably well-organized command chain and its residual neutral status to accelerate the reconciliation process. A clear policy framework was necessary for such an endeavor to be implemented at scale.

In the context of the development of the reconciliation principles and in support of government-led reconciliation, UNAMA has reiterated this offer to use its good offices to conduct political contact work with insurgency-related networks. But without unambiguous government endorsement, the reality is that international organization must be extremely cautious in committing itself to such support work. There have been multiple examples of real or imagined international contacts with elements of the insurgency being conspiratorially interpreted by both government and nongovernment Afghan actors, which act as a significant disincentive to any cautious institution in pursuing bona fide reconciliation support work.

Alongside UNAMA, the Provincial Reconstruction Teams (PRTs) are the other part of the international presence that could have been expected to contribute to reconciliation. The PRTs are mixed military-civilian teams deployed at the provincial level to undertake assistance and capacity-building programs and contribute to security. In reality, the PRTs have found themselves generally unable to make a significant contribution to reconciliation. They are constrained both by the lack of a consistent and transparent government approach to reconciliation, which the PRTs could have supported and comple- mented, and by the PRTs' own staffing profile, which may not include appropriate interlocutors.

Back-Channel Tracks

The minimalist international involvement in reconciliation-oriented contacts with both insurgent networks and those who can influence them is perplexing, particularly given the internationalization of the conflict. There is a major international strategic commitment to the battlefield, which international forces engage in directly. In terms of the rhetoric of the conflict, insurgents consistently articulate the presence or actions of international forces as principal reasons for fighting, even where political analysis indicates that the underlying reason for the fighting is intra-Afghan disputes. And yet, since 2001, internationally led political dialogue with the armed opposition and the promotion of reconciliation has essentially been off the agenda.

There is an obvious potential tension between the Afghan govern- ment and its international partners on the issue of top-level contacts with insurgents. The government has sought to monopolize these contacts, asserting its sovereign right, while politically striving to use any progress to shore up its own position. In this sense, the government-insurgent track represents the search for Pashtoon allies in a complex domestic-power balancing act. Given the partisan dimension of such a process and the poor prospects of any significant insurgents embracing such an alliance, such a track is a doubtful guarantee that legitimate international interests are being addressed.

The principal international interests in pursuit of reconciliation with Afghan insurgents are how to delink insurgents from al-Qaida, obtain credible guarantees against the use of Afghanistan or Pakistan for international terrorism, and win cooperation in the process of stabilizing Afghanistan under a cooperative dispensation. A viable way to ensure that the international concerns are addressed would be to develop an appropriate direct contact track with the Taliban leadership (*Quetta shura*) to seek agreement on the exclusion of international terrorism and the role of Afghan and international forces. The rationale for such an engagement would be that provisional agreement on this track would be a prerequisite for international support to the Afghan-Afghan track in which the Afghan parties discuss the terms of inclusion of insurgents into the political system.

However, the reality is that a formidable set of factors militate against any comprehensive settlement, even if the international security and domestic inclusion issues could be sequenced. Insiders to the current Kabul-based government, al-Qaida, Pakistani jihadis, and ideological insurgents would all see incentives to sabotage any reconciliation process. The configuration of international stakeholders leaves no single party with the authority to represent international concerns or the capacity to engage such a track. Any process seeking to engage at the level of the Quetta shura becomes vulnerable to sabotage, because any insurgent figure taking a pragmatic stance in a shura process risks exposing himself to accusations of collaboration. A possible response to the limited prospects of a comprehensive agreement would be to use a flexible back-channel approach that engaged different nodes of the Taliban leadership, with an option either to develop the dialogue segmentally and pragmatically by inviting amenable commander networks toward the government's reconciliation and reintegration apparatus or to develop the dialogue comprehensively and politically whenever support for such an option is viable within the insurgency leadership.

A related international dimension to engagement with insurgents is the role of Pakistan. Pakistan's declared support for reconciliation, in the form of long-standing calls for the Taliban to be allowed to join the political process, remains untested. As part of the pursuit of an engagement track with insurgents, the international sponsors of the process in Afghanistan should seek Islamabad's endorsement of the idea of locating some level of this political dialogue within Pakistan. All the most important commander networks involved in the insurgency have a presence in Pakistan and are potentially accessible for dialogue in a way that is not practicable within the conflict zone. Given the decentralized nature of the insurgency relative to the old Islamic Emirate structures, which operated in the period when the United Nations led negotiations in the 1990s, the freedom to operate in Pakistan would be a significant advantage for any reconciliation-political dialogue. The facilitation of such a decentralized approach would allow some prospect of breaking the monopoly of spoilers on engagement. Furthermore, Pakistan could legitimately seek reassurances regarding its own security interests in blessing such a dialogue, and given its declared preference for political approaches to insurgency, accepting such an international request would be consistent with its declared policy stance.

The Saudi Process

In September 2008, Saudi Arabia initiated political dialogue with a range of Afghan political actors, initially within the space provided by the kingdom's traditional Ramadan hospitality. The dialogue involved discussion among Saudi representatives, close political allies of the Afghan government, and prominent Kabul-based former Taliban leaders. In addition, the Saudi leadership was successful in winning the participation of Afghans close to the Quetta-based Taliban leadership, enabling the first steps of a meaningful probe of Taliban political objectives. The prestige of Saudi Arabia within Afghanistan was a significant factor in securing high-level participation in the process. The enthusiastic engagement of the Afghan government was significant because the process has had more substantive content than the previous largely rhetorical presidential initiatives. Although the dialogue covered much of the ground that would be hoped for in any international back-channel track, unsurprisingly no agreement has been forthcoming and the official Taliban position remains that no talks have taken place. However, feedback from various insurgent networks indicates that the Saudi process has helped to shift attitudes within the insurgency in favor of the idea of engagement and against what is widely perceived as the intransigence of the insurgency's leadership.

8

The Musa Qala Accord

The Musa Qala Accord, which was signed in September 2006, arose as a response to a military exigency and became a vehicle for the provincial administration to reengage politically with beleaguered and estranged tribes. Although it represents the most prominent recent example of Afghans drawing on traditional Afghan institutions for reconciliation, with echoes of the old methods of frontier politics, it provides a revealing case study of both the opportunities and the pitfalls in pursuing nonviolent approaches to managing the Afghan conflict and offers valuable lessons for both the Afghan government and its international supporters. It also provides a classic example of how a lack of strategy and coherence in decision making can have disastrous effects on the ability of government to successfully use political initiatives. Although the tribal elders involved in the Musa Qala Accord were momentarily successful in extricating their town from the conflict, the chronic failure of government organs and their international counterparts to support the tribally backed administration that had been installed in Musa Qala, along with the undermining of the political backing for the accord in Kabul, meant that the Taliban were able to relatively easily overrun the district center within just six months of the accord's signing.

The Tribal Political Context of the Accord

In terms of tribal structure, Musa Qala is dominated by two of the branches of the Alizai tribe, the Hassanzai and Pirzai. In the first four years of the Bonn process, the government relied upon the family of Sher Mohammad Akhundzada, which belongs to the Hassanzai branch and was originally based in the historically important area of Zamindawar, close to Musa Qala, to stabilize Helmand province. Sher Mohammad served as provincial governor until October 2005 and his brother, Amir Mohammad, served initially as Musa Qala's district administrator and then as deputy governor after Sher Mohammad was appointed to the Senate. Sher Mohammad's uncle, Nassim Akhundzada, was a prominent figure in Helmand and the southwest during the jihad era. While recognized as one of the leading political families in the southwestern region, the Akhundzadas had accumulated multiple local feuds, not least because of a famous incident in which Nassim ordered the summary execution of most of the traditional Alizai tribal leadership in northern Helmand.

The development of the post-2001 insurgency in Musa Qala followed the classic pattern of the southern provinces. The district administrator, Amir Mohammad, and the local commanders personally affiliated to him engaged in predatory behavior, such as capturing control of heroin-trafficking routes between northern Helmand and the Pakistani and Iranian borders. The violent attempts by Amir Mohammad and his associates to monopolize power in Musa Qala and benefit from the heroin trade alienated much of the Alizai tribe. A prominent example of this alienation is provided by Tor Jan Pirzai, one of the more infamous local Taliban commanders. After the fall of the Taliban regime, Tor Jan worked as a tailor in the Musa Qala bazaar. He was arrested and beaten on the orders of then district administrator Amir Mohammad. Upon his release, Tor Jan adopted the epithet "mullah" and joined the armed opposition as one of its most active commanders. Other victims of the new administration's arbitrary arrests, searches, and taxation, and of its opium politics either followed Tor Jan into the armed opposition or at least became estranged from the government.

With the elevation of Sher Mohammad to the Senate, the central government appeared to accept in late 2005 the analysis that the narrow tribal base and predatory approach of the Helmand administration was actually an impediment to stabilization. In turn, the new governor, Daud, hoped to be able to rebuild the relationship between the government and the estranged tribal factions.

The Military Context of the Accord

The Musa Qala Accord had both a military and a political logic. Contrary to the hopes that the installation of a provincial governor who was not associated with any of the jihad-era feuds in Helmand would help stabilize the province, the arrival of Governor Daud and the initial deployment of the British ISAF detachment were accompanied by an escalation in insurgency violence in Helmand. There were three main factors behind the intensification of conflict in Helmand. First, what happened in Helmand in 2006 paralleled what was happening in the rest of southern Afghanistan, as Taliban tried to step up their attacks in all provinces in which they were active. Second, commanders in Helmand with links to the Akhundzada network who had hitherto been dormant or focused on trafficking were encouraged by Sher Mohammad's departure to side with the Taliban. And, most crucially, third, the British deployment of small detachments in "platoon houses" in the outlying districts provided an opportunity for local Taliban to mobilize around a battle against the "traditional enemy" (the British). Instead of backing up the Afghan National Security Forces (ANSF) and stabilizing the district, the British platoon house became something of a magnet for attacks. As a result, the ISAF presence in Musa Qala was maintained at high cost with no obvious military advantage, and the persistent fighting precluded any possibility of the provincial administration pushing ahead with its planned political process of reengaging the previously estranged Pirzai and dissident elements of the Hassanzai.

The Contents of the Accord

The accord consisted of a fourteen-point written agreement between the Helmand provincial governor and a fifteen-man district tribal *jirga*, headed by Shah Agha. It provided for the tribal elders' *jirga* to support a district administration that would fly the Afghan flag. According to the agreement, the *jirga* was to nominate fifty men to be trained and recruited into the Afghanistan National Auxiliary Police (ANAP) to maintain security in the district center and along the main road. With *jirga* backing, the local administration was to provide security for nongovernmental organizations (NGOs) and civilian departments working in the district and to assure the safe transit of national and international military forces. The *jirga* guaranteed that the district would not be used for military operations against other areas. Only the police (that is, the trained local security force) were to be allowed to bear arms in the district center. The *jirga* was to supervise the collection of local revenue, propose spending plans to the provincial government, and help keep the district schools open. The unwritten clause of the accord was that its provisions would apply within a five-kilometer radius of the district center. Thus, in effect, the *jirga* was expected to not exert its authority beyond this distance and ISAF forces were expected to stay out of the district center but would remain free to conduct operations beyond the five-kilometer limit. Although the formal agreement was between the Afghan government and the Musa Qala tribal elders, it was clear that, to be able to deliver on their undertakings in this agreement, the elders conducted their own contacts with the local Taliban. In these contacts, the elders instructed the Taliban to call off their attacks on the district and stay out of the five-kilometer zone. In terms of composition, the *jirga* membership included a balance between Hassanzai and Pirzai, in line with the population of the district center. Subsequent background checks of the *jirga* members indicated that they were mostly credible tribal elders and not obvious proxies or stooges of the different factions or drug mafias active in Helmand politics.

The Outcome of the Accord

In September 2006, the *jirga*-backed tribal administration began to run Musa Qala under the terms of the accord. ISAF forces withdrew from the district, and the previous local police contingent, which had existed under Amir Mohammad's administration, evaporated. The governor appointed local figures as district police chief and district administrator on the basis of recommendations from the *jirga*. The *jirga* nominated men for recruitment to ANAP and sent them off to Lashkargah for training. However, there were delays in processing them and by February 2007 the district administration only had nineteen auxiliary police at its disposal.

For a five-month period, there was a lull in fighting in Musa Qala. Taliban respected the ban on entering the bazaar, which had reopened for business, and the *jirga* succeeded in turning them back the first time that a commander tried to enter with arms. The three government schools and several informal mosque schools reopened and operated relatively normally, and there were no significant security incidents within the area covered by the accord.

Shah Agha and his *jirga* engaged in an intensive public relations campaign, traveling to Lashkargah and Kabul to reassure stakeholders that they were a bona fide district *jirga* and to canvass support for the accord. However, their repeated attempts to persuade provincial-level department heads from the line ministries to visit Musa Qala failed. Likewise, multiple promises of "quick impact" assistance for the district resulted in protracted subcontract negotiations and little sign of work or cash injection into Musa Qala. The *jirga* acknowledged receiving one vehicle from the government as a token of support for the initiative.

During the winter of 2006–2007, the Musa Qala Accord became a major focus of controversy. The NDS circulated a briefing that erroneously described the accord as an agreement that had been signed by the British Army and the Taliban. Numerous reports circulated in Kabul that suggested that the Taliban had established a parallel court in the district, that questioned whether the Afghanistan or Taliban flag was flying, and that implied that the accord had turned Musa Qala into a haven for insurgents on a par with Waziristan. Additionally, the PAG discussed the Musa Qala issue several times and debated whether the accord constituted a dilution of Afghan sovereignty because of the lack of a fully fledged court and prosecution service. But such debates and discussions were largely disconnected from the reality on the ground. Anyone familiar with conditions in the south at that time appreciated that these institutions were barely functional in any of the districts of Helmand and Kandahar. The PAG ultimately decided to perform a test and have ANSF and ISAF forces transit through the district in accordance with the transit provision of the accord.

Meanwhile, in a thinly disguised criticism of the conduct of affairs in Helmand and of the close cooperation between the British PRT and the provincial governor, the president sacked Daud in December 2006 and appointed Asadullah Wafa in his place. The new governor announced his intention to renegotiate the accord to strengthen the role of central government. He produced an amended version of the text, saying that the *jirga* would have to accept the government's appointment of officials on merit and that the *jirga* would have to hand over collected revenue to the provincial administration. But such issues became moot in February 2007, when an ISAF airstrike on a house outside the five-kilometer zone killed one of the Taliban district commanders, prompting his brother to enter the district center in force and declare a resumption of the jihad against foreign forces. The Taliban soon disarmed the district security officials, placed the *jirga* under house arrest, and occupied the district center. They remained there until a major ISAF and Afghan National Army (ANA) operation expelled them in December 2007. In the end, a new district administration was installed under former Taliban commander Mullah Abdul Salaam without any supporting accord.

Lessons from the Accord

The experience of the Musa Qala Accord suggests several lessons—both for the Afghan government and international supporters—that should be used to guide future initiatives that seek to end local conflict through agreements with community leaders or amenable Taliban.

Anticipate Controversy. Any reconciliation initiative holds immense potential for controversy, even when Taliban involvement is only indirect. Such controversies tend to have a momentum of their own, divorced from the reality and significance of the original issue. In the case of Musa Qala, much of the debate around the accord seemed to be divorced from the reality of governance and tribal relationships in insurgency-affected districts. The debate also exaggerated the differences between the ways in which the Helmand authorities dealt with conflict in Musa Qala and the range of pragmatic approaches employed in other beleaguered districts. Furthermore, the rather acrimonious debate over whether the Musa Qala Accord constituted an infringement of Afghan sovereignty distracted attention from the important operational issue of whether the tribal elders involved had adequate leverage over and autonomy from the Taliban. In turn, the intensity of the debate undermined political backing for the accord in Kabul and made it more difficult to garner the assistance needed to strengthen the hand of the tribal *jirga*.

Engage Tribal Leadership. Musa Qala demonstrated the existence of a viable local tribal leadership that was prepared, when given the right backing, to stake its personal prestige on working with the government to establish administrative and security arrangements. For the duration of the accord, the leaders proved willing and able to exert influence over insurgents to keep conflict out of the district center. The credentials of Shah Agha and his associates in the *jirga* came under minute scrutiny, with critics trying to establish that they were merely stooges for the Taliban. However, a fair judgment seems to be that the fifteen individuals were broadly representative of the tribal mix in central Musa Qala and thus were able to mobilize all tribes and subtribes in the area and to apply social pressure to the Taliban. The *jirga* was an effective way of reengaging Pirzai with the administration. Although no major Taliban figures ended their hostilities in response to the accord, a tentative UN assessment indicated that "non-ideological local Taliban," who had been estranged from the previous local administration, did respond positively to the overtures from Shah Agha's *jirga*.[1] The fact that the local party to the accord was a tribal *jirga* preempted one of the familiar problems with such arrangements—that they can confer some legitimacy on an insurgent organization. The underlying logic of the deal was a quid pro quo in which the government would keep international security forces out of the district center and the tribal elders would achieve through peaceful means what the forces were supposed to be doing—excluding the Taliban. Such a deal offered armed insurgents neither practical advantage nor legitimacy.

Deliver Timely Tangible Benefits. The Afghan government and international support structures are too chronically cumbersome to deliver quick impact projects or capacity-building assistance to a challenging environment like Musa Qala. Of the many dimensions to this problem, the difficulty of relating operationally to informal structures such as the Musa Qala *jirga* is but one. The range of stakeholders were happy to talk with a *jirga*, but all expected to channel resources through government departments, which in reality were never going to set foot in Musa Qala. In effect, the government and international community left the Musa Qala *jirga* high and dry. As the local sponsors of the deal, Shah Agha and the *jirga* were expected to use their influence on other local actors to advocate compliance. To do this successfully, they needed to be able to deliver tangible benefits in the district center to acquire and use some power of patronage and, through the district police and links to security forces outside the district, to mobilize at least a minimal force to defend the district.

---

1. UNAMA, "*Assessment of the Effects of the Musa Qala Agreement*" (internal memo, UNAMA, Kabul, January 2007).

Instead, projects remained bogged down in bureaucratic delays and support to the auxiliary police was inflexible. All the *jirga* received from the new governor was more undelivered promises and demands to submit to central authority on the appointment of government personnel to the district and to hand over local revenue to the provincial administration. Such demands were in any case largely tokenistic as the provincial administration had few personnel willing to serve in Musa Qala and had little expectation of receiving revenue from the district. Whereas there was a need to enhance the prestige of the tribesmen working with the accord, the handling of the follow-up by the government and international community seemed calculated to undermine them.

Support the Local Partners. Politics is everything, especially in reconciliation, and a good idea is of little use unless there is a robust political strategy to support it. This lesson is relevant for sponsors of any future reconciliation initiative. Long before the Taliban forced their way back into Musa Qala, "court politics" had fatally undermined the confidence of the Afghan government in the arrangements through which Musa Qala was being administered. The key stakeholders involved in the intensive and insidious lobbying against the accord included parts of the NDS, partisans of the former provincial governor, and members of the presidential entourage. Between them they suggested that Afghan sovereignty had been compromised, that the accord was linked to Pakistani General Pervez Musharraf's use of accords in Waziristan, and that, in effect, the process amounted to a willful capitulation to the Taliban. Despite a paucity of evidence to support these positions, the president showed himself to be sympathetic to them.

Although the president stopped short of actually canceling the accord, the systematic undermining of political support for it in Kabul was significant for the outcome because of the role of informal linkages in the process. Success in Musa Qala depended upon boosting the prestige of fifteen tribal elders so that they could have maximum leverage over the range of other actors in the district. For this to happen, it was important that everyone know that the *jirga* enjoyed access to and cooperation from government departments and the institutions with the capacity to help in the district. It was important that the *jirga* be able to deliver more effective, timely support for their new district police force than could ever be expected through unreliable Ministry of Interior structures. But by January 2007, both the *jirga* and the government departments that should have been supporting it had received ample messages that the accord was an unwelcome child.

It is somewhat ironic that when the 2008 U.S. Intelligence Estimate reported that the Afghan government controlled only 30 percent of the national territory,[2] the director of the NDS became the most articulate exponent of the position that effective cooperation between the government and loyal tribes would be the key to stability in Afghanistan, arguing that such cooperation would compensate for limited direct government control—the very logic underlying the Musa Qala Accord.

Overall Assessment

Setting aside the conspiratorial criticisms of Musa Qala, the issue of whether it constituted a potentially useful reconciliation initiative rests on whether there was a genuine intention to "restore relations" as a sustainable basis for ending conflict or whether both sides hoped to use the accord tactically, pausing the fight to gather strength for the next round. The efforts of the *jirga*—at no small risk to its members—over the six months of the accord indicate that it was committed to extricating Musa Qala from the conflict. The *jirga*'s efforts constituted significant local ownership. Shah Agha and his men successfully ended gun battles in the district center for six months and restored a degree of normal life. While it lasted, the impact was positive. The problem was that support for the accord was not robust enough to enable the *jirga* to deflect or deter a reactive Taliban incursion into the town.

The restoration of relationships attempted under the accord was more subtle than the simple idea of remorseful combatants laying down arms. The *jirga* made good use of the challenge to end the firefight around the platoon house by involving the tribes in support of the administration. The real reconciliation that they effected was with those who had been estranged by the early years of Afghanistan's post-2001 predatory rule. As long as the government backed the *jirga* process and

---

2. J. Michael McConnell, *Annual Threat Assessment of the Intelligence Community for the Senate Armed Services Committee* (Washington, DC: Senate Armed Services Committee, February 2008).

its balance between Hassanzai and Pirzai, this aspect of reconciliation was viable. The accord did not claim to make committed insurgents foreswear violence. In fact, given the trend across the rest of the south, it probably would have been unrealistic to try to achieve this through such an accord. The accord also demonstrated government and international partner flexibility and commitment to a peaceful resolution of local conflict and their ability to engage with local actors. Thus, the accord had the potential to contribute to a de-escalation of the conflict, something that in itself does not constitute reconciliation but is necessary in preparing the ground for it.

During the six months of the accord, there was no evidence of the Taliban exploiting it strategically. The couple of verified incidents of Taliban "probing" were minor. Before February 2007, the ISAF was able to operate in the district outside the five-kilometer zone without collapsing the accord. And local Taliban commanders carried on largely as before but without access to the district center. The strategic buildup of Taliban in Musa Qala came only after the collapse of the accord. Even so, the relative ease with which the ISAF moved back into the district in December 2007 indicates that this Taliban buildup was highly ineffectual. The question that will remain unanswered is whether the district could have turned the Taliban back after the February 2007 missile strike if the *jirga* had been properly supported.

9

Key Findings and Recommendations

Reconciliation in the Bonn Context

- It is now widely understood that the Bonn Accords did not constitute a peace agreement. They needed to be supplemented by a strategic pursuit of reconciliation in order to bring all Afghan parties to the conflict into the peaceful political process.
- To date, support for even the most restrictive versions of reconciliation has been inadequate and undermined by a lack of consistent political backing and inadequate oversight and coordination.
- As a measure of how slow progress has been, only 12 out of the 142 senior Taliban figures found on the UN Security Council sanctions list have so far reconciled, along with 10 other figures of equivalent rank who were not on the UN list.
- The lack of effective commitment to reconciliation means that potential allies are turned into enemies and that the government must rely excessively on military force, for which it ultimately turns to its international allies. In turn, this excessive dependence on military force, especially by international forces, risks undermining both the internal and external legitimacy of the international intervention in Afghanistan and the political system that intervention purports to support.
- A further consequence of the lack of progress on reconciliation is that opportunities to split elements within the insurgency who are uncomfortable with terror tactics from those who endorse the use of such tactics have not been taken advantage of.
- If blame must be accorded for the absence of peace and reconciliation in Afghanistan, the first to be blamed should be the insurgency leaders who failed to take advantage of genuine opportunities to participate in the post-Bonn process, who have plunged their country into an avoidable new conflict, and who have themselves made no contribution to a political settlement. However, the basic culpability

of the insurgent leaders and their sponsors should not distract the Afghan government and international community from their own responsibility to pursue reconciliation.

Barriers to Reconciliation in the Post-Bonn Context

- Key opportunities to lay the groundwork for reconciliation were missed in the early stages of the post-2001 international engagement in Afghanistan.
- Afghanistan currently faces a full-scale insurgency that includes both Afghan elements committed to sustaining the conflict indefinitely and non-Afghan jihadis and regional sponsors opposed to the very basis of the existing political order in Afghanistan. Within this context, there is no imminent prospect of progress on any reconciliation track that aims to achieve a comprehensive negotiated political settlement and a discrete end to the conflict.
- An insider-outsider dynamic has also acted as a deterrent to reconciliation. Stakeholders in the system of government established after Bonn have at times strengthened their position by fomenting conflict, exploiting the rhetoric of the "war on terror," and blocking opportunities for estranged groups to join the new order. They have pursued individual and factional advantage at the expense of creating the required conditions for peace and stability.
- The requirements of strengthening its domestic political support have at times acted as an incentive for the Karzai administration to pursue reconciliation. However, the de facto requirement that those reconciling must specifically associate themselves with the administration rather than more broadly accept the political system probably acts as a disincentive for members of the armed opposition to enter reconciliation.
- The absence of any political wing of the Taliban—or of any other part of the armed opposition—complicates the reconciliation process. In consequence, the government lacks legitimate interlocutors and the insurgents lack patrons or representatives whom they would trust to safeguard their legitimate dealings with the government.

- Any strategically pursued reconciliation program would be very demanding on government capacity in terms of the requirements for sustained, collective action.

Opportunities for Reconciliation and the Terms of Reconciliation

- Even in the absence of the needed conditions for a negotiated settlement, there are opportunities to promote forms of reconciliation that could lead toward an incremental peace in which the intensity of conflict is reduced by enabling some conflict actors to enter the political process and in which the conditions for peace are created.

- In terms of political content, reconciliation arrangements range from subjugation, co-option, and accommodation to appeasement and capitulation. To date, the focus of the Afghan government and international partners has been primarily on achieving subjugation or co-option of the armed opposition. But these efforts have achieved little strategic effect, partly because the fear of appeasement or capitulation has been used to deter potentially effective measures of accommodation.

- To date, remarkably few middle- or senior-level figures involved in the post-2001 insurgency have reconciled. One of the biggest opportunities to ensure that reconciliation efforts contribute to peace involves redirecting efforts to engage meaningfully with those actually driving the conflict—that is, the leadership of the different networks comprising the insurgency.

- Pursuing political dialogue, championing justice and human rights, and addressing the root causes of the conflict all contribute to a holistic process of reconciliation. However, post-Bonn official channels of reconciliation were robbed at an early stage of such a process and have been reduced to pursuing a security-dominated version of reconciliation.

- Afghanistan has a rich heritage of traditions and institutions related to conflict avoidance and resolution upon which actors in the current conflict have drawn and that can provide authentic local content for any reconciliation program.

- The accommodation of a credible faction of Hezb-i-Islami in the political system represents a notable positive step in reconciliation.
- Even the most effective reconciliation measures can serve only as components of the broader strategy. In particular, they must be complemented by improvements in governance and the effective deployment of Afghan security forces, which can help ensure the security of those accepting the political order.
- In the absence of a comprehensive settlement, reconciliation measures will remain a complement to military action and security measures—not a substitute for them.
- No serious, sustained attempt has yet been made to solicit the cooperation of Pakistan in supporting reconciliation in Afghanistan. Rather, the focus of requests to Pakistan has been on security measures. Pakistan's expressed preference for political approaches to conflict should provide opportunities to pursue reconciliation with amenable parts of the Afghan insurgent networks based in Pakistan.

Recommendations for the Afghan Government

- Adopt an unambiguous strategy of promotion of reconciliation as the preferred way out of the current conflict.
- Support the renewed commitment to reconciliation with serious strategic planning and management, a clear assignment of roles and resources, a well-defined program for monitoring progress, and a willingness to adjust course as necessary.
- Acknowledge the importance and legitimacy of accommodation as a route to reconciliation in addition to co-option or subjugation and reflect this in the updated version of the reconciliation principles. Allocate political responsibility within the administration for setting the parameters of any accommodation reached with insurgent elements amenable to reconciliation through this route. Ensure that postreconciliation monitoring arrangements cover the adherence of all sides to their commitments.
- Pursue a nonpartisan approach to reconciliation, ensuring that reconciliation is framed as a mechanism through which individuals can extricate themselves from armed opposition to the current political

order and not simply as a mechanism through which individuals submit to the administration. Seek consensus support for reconciliation on this basis from the key political and civil-society stakeholders, including the lawful opposition, and take action against administration allies who undermine the reconciliation process.

- Build public and political class support by clearly articulating what the government seeks to achieve through reconciliation. Maximize transparency, portray reconciliation achievements realistically, and actively combat attempts to equate reconciliation with appeasement or to describe it as a conspiracy.

- Help create the space for the emergence of legitimate interlocutors for those within the insurgency who are amenable to reconciliation. The interlocutors should be enabled to articulate their counterparts' key concerns, to establish confidence as a basis for entry into reconciliation, and to protect the insurgents in the process of reintegration.

- Revamp the official apparatus for support of reconciliation by assigning operational responsibility for politically significant reconciliation to a credible agency capable of participating in strategic management. In appointing a "senior focal point" for reconciliation, ensure that he is empowered to initiate collective action to promote reconciliation through security, administrative, and economic support measures.

- Take note of what has worked to date and apply lessons learned to best ensure the practical implementation of reconciliation.

- Reinforce the role of the subnational administration as the key arm of government charged with facilitating the peaceful reintegration of reconciled former combatants.

- Proactively solicit the Pakistan government for cooperation in launching dialogue with those elements in the insurgency who are most accessible in Pakistan and who are amenable to reconciliation.

- Task the "senior focal point" to unify the different efforts toward reconciliation by exploiting synergies between the security-oriented strand, the justice and reconciliation strand, and the local peace-building strand.

Recommendations for the International Community

- Ensure that efforts in support of reconciliation are fully coordinated and take place within the strategy framework agreed upon with the Afghan government.
- Task UNAMA with using its good offices, outreach network, and analytical capacity to pursue reconciliation contacts as part of this strategy.
- Ensure that there is a clear focal point in all PRTs and relevant combat formations capable of establishing and maintaining contacts with those insurgents amenable to reconciliation. Ensure that such contacts are appropriately coordinated with relevant parts of the Afghan government.
- Support reconciliation smartly, ensuring that progress toward objectives is monitored and used as a basis for planning and extending support.
- Conduct public information campaigns in support of reconciliation.
- Maintain direct contact channels to insurgency leaders with a view to preparing the ground for an eventual comprehensive approach to peace. Such contacts should be consistent with commitments implied in the reconciliation operating principles to ensure that reconciliation is coordinated.
- Actively combat attempts to sabotage bona fide reconciliation efforts—particularly if sabotage is in the form of disinformation campaigns conducted by regime insiders.
- Condition continued military and nonmilitary assistance to Afghanistan on the sustained pursuit by the Afghan government of an agreed-upon strategy to achieve peace, of which one element is reconciliation of the armed opposition.

Appendix A

List of Reconciled Middle- and Senior-Level Taliban Figures, 2001–2008

Name	UN Sanctions List No.	Former Designation	Place of Birth	Route Back	PTS
Ustad Akbari	Not listed	Adviser Hazarajat	Bamyan	Political sponsorship	NO
Abdul Wahid Baghrani	Not listed	Military Commander	Helmand	Executive intervention	NO
Habibullah Fauzi	TI.F.124.01	First Secretary Islamabad Embassy	Ghazni	Political sponsorship and Parliament	YES
Sufi Gardezi	Not listed	Military Commander	Pakita	Political sponsorship	NO
Nur Ali Haidery	Not listed	Director Ariana Afghan Airlines	Kandahar	Political sponsorship	NO
Musa Hotak	TI.H.65.01	Deputy Minister Planning	Maidan		NO
Mawlvi Islam	TI.M.90.01	Govenor Bamyan	Samangan	Political sponsorship and Parliament	NO
Abdul Samad Khaksar	TI.K.54.01	Deputy Minister Interior	Kandahar	Political sponsorship	NO
Naeem Kochai	Not listed	Military Commander	Logar	Detention and executive order	NO
Abdul Hakeem Mujahid	TI.M.116.01	Envoy to the UN	Paktika	Political sponsorship	YES
Mullah Mujahid	Not listed	Military Commander	Urozgan	Detention and executive order	NO

Name	UN Sanctions List No.	Former Designation	Place of Birth	Route Back	PTS
Abdul Hakeem Munib	TI.M.41.01	Deputy Minister Public Works	Pakita	Loya Jirga	NO
Wakil Hakeem Mutawakil	TI.M.32.01	Minister Foreign Affairs	Kandahar	Detention and political sponsorship	NO
Ishaq Nizami	Not listed	Director Radio Shariat	Nangarhar	PTS and executive sponsorship	YES
Mawlvi Qalamuddin	TI.M.74.01	Deputy Minister Vice and Virtue	Logar	PTS and parliamentary election	YES
Mawlvi Arsala Rahmani	TI.R.46.01	Minister of Higher Education	Paktika	Political sponsorship	YES
Abdul Salaam Rocketi	Not listed	Core Commander	Zabul	Political sponsorship and parliament	NO
Abdul Salaam	Not listed	Governor	Helmand	Executive intervention	NO
Rahmatullah Sangaryar	Not listed	Military Commander	Urozgan	Detention and executive order	NO
Jalaludin Shinwary	TI.S.59.01	Deputy Minister Justice	Nangarhar	Political sponsorship	NO
Rahmatullah Wahidyar	TI.W.76.01	Deputy Minister Martyrs	Paktia	Political sponsorship	YES
Abdul Salaam Zaeef	TI.Z.62.01	Ambassador to Pakistan	Kandahar	Detention and executive order	YES

Appendix B

Comparative Analysis of Afghan Reconciliation Initiatives

Parameters	Reconciliation Initiatives	
	NSC diplomacy	PTS
Standing of those reconciled	Mainly middle- and senior-level figures, including those who have either been active in the insurgency or are in a position to influence elements of the insurgency, have been targeted.	Although it is intended for middle-level Taliban leaders and active insurgents, very few of either category have joined the program. Mainly long-retired mujahideen and insignificant noncombatants have participated in it.
Transparency	The process is discrete verging on the opaque; NSC engagement with insurgent networks is not normally acknowledged as a formal program and reporting is not in the public domain.	Reconciliation is a public process and is reported.
Terms of the bargain	NSC deals with reconciling figures are custom-made. The spirit is one of co-option; reconcilers are pressured to acknowledge publicly their submission to the government. However, the NSC has latitude to offer appropriate terms for its clients, which could amount to accommodation.	Clients are offered liberty and a promise of nonharassment in return for accepting the political order, which equals subjugation.
Inclusiveness	The process targets individuals.	The program works with individuals. Provincial offices have occasionally delivered organized groups of fighters who reportedly made a collective decision to affiliate themselves with the government.
Instruments	The process employs contacts, political dialogue, discretionary assistance, and referrals.	The program offers certification and a basic ritual of reconciliation in the form of a hearing with jihadi veteran and spiritual figure Sebghatullah Mojadedi.

Parameters	Reconciliation Initiatives	
	NSC diplomacy	PTS
International dimension	The NSC has drawn on international funding, coordinated some security assessments with international agencies, and made some use of international "good offices" in its contact work. Otherwise the process is entirely Afghan.	Internationals fund and encourage the program and have attempted to provide capacity-building support, although they have no real political role and do nothing to help the commission approach insurgent networks.

	Reconciliation principles	Hezb-i-Islami track	Governor-led reconciliation
Standing of those reconciled	The process has not yet been implemented. It is intended for bona fide insurgent-related figures.	This track focuses on political leaders and former senior commanders with strong links to at least one element of the insurgency.	Such initiatives tend to focus on significant, active insurgents and those who can influence them. Governors have specifically targeted insurgent figures whom they consider critical to the security of their province.
Transparency	It is essentially a transparent political process, but it provides for confidentially as required to protect clients.	Political agreement was legalized in the form of the Justice Ministry's registration of the faction. Rapprochement was backed up by covert assistance.	It is a political and potentially transparent process, but it is not systematically reported on because governors are under-managed. Governors have the potential to commission covert work, particularly in those situations where the governor has a functional relationship with the provincial NDS chief.

Parameters	Reconciliation Initiatives		
	Reconciliation principles	Hezb-i-Islami track	Governor-led reconciliation
Terms of the bargain	It is based explicitly on co-option.	Although Hezb-i-Islami was simply allowed to operate under the same rules as others, the political engagement generated a significant reduction in persecution of Hezb veterans and led to the induction of Hezb figures into the administration—that is, the arrangement went beyond co-option to accommodation.	Governors are in a position to address grievances regarding administrative and security arrangements, so terms are flexible. Past practice includes examples of accommodation.
Inclusiveness	It is open to all willing insurgents, but in practice it will likely cover only selected individuals, as there is no provision to make it accessible to whole networks.	The political agreement involved an entire faction, represented by its leadership.	These efforts are relatively inclusive; governors have wooed both key individuals and networks.
Instruments	It is a revamped version of the PTS.	The political agreement was achieved initially through the use of discrete dialogue and later through publicly acknowledged dialogue, financial support, the authorization of political activity, and the establishment of links with the executive.	Governors employ tribal diplomacy and jirgas, give offers of amnesty and cooperation, and address local grievances.

Parameters	Reconciliation Initiatives		
	Reconciliation principles	Hezb-i-Islami track	Governor-led reconciliation
International dimension	Internationals are expected to support it financially. The only operational involvement from them is the offer of UNAMA's good offices.	There has been significant international involvement; Hezb leadership sought and received international endorsement for rapprochement.	There has been little international involvement in the governors' initiatives. Some governors choose to associate PRT lead nations with their local initiatives in a peripheral role.

Index

United States Institute of Peace Press

Since its inception, the United States Institute of Peace Press has published over 150 books on the prevention, management, and peaceful resolution of international conflicts—among them such venerable titles as Raymond Cohen's *Negotiating Across Cultures; Herding Cats* and *Leashing the Dogs of War* by Chester A. Crocker, Fen Osler Hampson, and Pamela Aall; and I. William Zartman's *Peacemaking and International Conflict.* All our books arise from research and fieldwork sponsored by the Institute's many programs. In keeping with the best traditions of scholarly publishing, each volume undergoes both thorough internal review and blind peer review by external subject experts to ensure that the research, scholarship, and conclusions are balanced, relevant, and sound. As the Institute prepares to move to its new headquarters on the National Mall in Washington, D.C., the Press is committed to extending the reach of the Institute's work by continuing to publish significant and sustainable works for practitioners, scholars, diplomats, and students.

VALERIE NORVILLE
DIRECTOR

Reconciliaion in Afghanistan

Text: Janson Text LT Std
Display Text: Bauer Bodoni
Cover Design: Kim Hasten/Katharine Moore
Page Layout: Cynthia Jordan
Developmental Editor: Kurt Volkan
Proofreading: Amanda Watson-Boles
Indexing: Potomac Indexing

DATE DUE

FEB 1 0 2011

JAN 0 2 2013

DEC 1 3 2010

APR 1 9 2011

FEB 1 0 2012

JAN 0 2 2013

MAR 0 5 2013